BUILDING
OUTDOOR
GEAR

Building
OUTDOOR
GEAR

Easy-to-Make Projects for Camping,
Fishing, Hunting, and Canoeing

REVISED SECOND EDITION

by GIL GILPATRICK

FOX CHAPEL
PUBLISHING

ISBN 978-1-56523-484-0

Library of Congress Cataloging-in-Publication Data

Gilpatrick, Gil.
Building outdoor gear / by Gil Gilpatrick. -- 2nd ed.
    p. cm.
Includes index.
ISBN 978-1-56523-484-0
1. Camping--Equipment and supplies--Design and construction. 2. Canoes and canoeing. 3. Sporting goods. I. Title.
GV191.76.G55 2012
796.5--dc23
                    2011029534

To learn more about the other great books from Fox Chapel Publishing, or to find a retailer near you, call toll-free 800-457-9112 or visit us at *www.FoxChapelPublishing.com.*

Note to Authors: We are always looking for talented authors to write new books
in our area of woodworking, design, and related crafts. Please send a brief letter
describing your idea to Acquisition Editor, 1970 Broad Street, East Petersburg, PA 17520.

Printed in China
First printing

ABOUT THE AUTHOR

Gil Gilpatrick has been a master Maine Guide for more than 40 years and has spent more than 30 of those years guiding parties on the Allagash and other of Maine's wilderness rivers. His experience on the Allagash has been gleaned from more than 100 trips through the waterway, guiding people from all walks of life. Gil was also an instructor of Outdoor Resources at the Skowhegan Regional Vocational Center, where he helped young people learn to live in and love the outdoors. A prolific writer with several outdoor books to his credit, Gil also writes a monthly column for Maine's *Northwoods Sporting Journal.* He is the 2010 recipient of the Legendary Maine Guide Award.

DEDICATION

To all my Outdoor Resources students during my years at the Skowhegan Regional Vocational Center who unwittingly helped me to produce this book.

THANKS

I would like to introduce my friends, Jason and Kelly Garland of Norridgewock, Maine. Jason was one of those students who helped me develop some of the projects in this book back in the early 1990s. Nearly 20 years later he emailed me asking if he and his wife, Kelly, could build a canoe in my shop. To make a long story short, they ended up making the strip canoe to illustrate the revised second edition of my book *Building A Strip Canoe*. With that project, they ended up owning a beautiful canoe, but then they graciously volunteered to help me with this second book even though they had no need for most of these projects. They came in after their day's work and put up with my demands for various photo angles, takes, and retakes. Thank you, folks—I am indebted to you.

CONTENTS

What You Can Make

32 **Canoe or Boat Seat**
These practical seats are the most comfortable way to spend all day sitting in a boat or canoe.

38 **Canoe Chair**
These have a long history in Maine; the back makes them a welcome treat on shore or for the third person in a canoe—and they're collapsible.

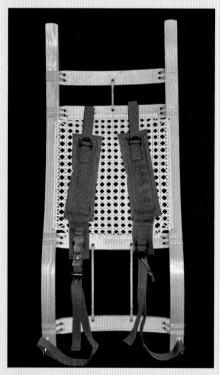

52 **Pack Frame**
With hardwood and nylon-fastened joints, these pack frames handle hard use much better than store-bought aluminum ones.

60 **Paddles**
I have not found a paddle that compares with these for strength, lightness, and flexibility.

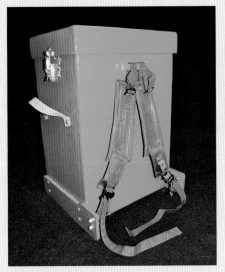

78 Trip Boxes
These boxes are tough, rainproof, roomy, and backpackable—I can't imagine packing for a trip without them.

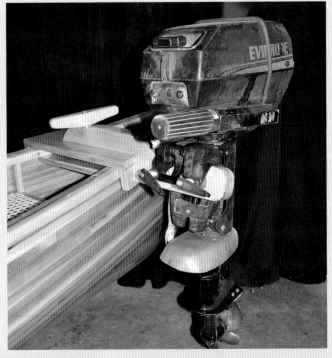

90 Canoe Motor Mount
"Universal" motor mounts don't work, in my experience—but you can make a hardy, custom mount perfect for your canoe.

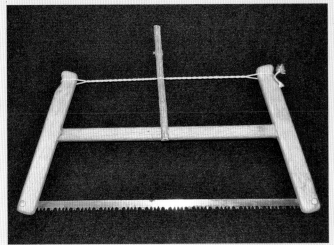

98 Bucksaw
A good saw is indispensable to the serious outdoorsperson; these two are both cheaper and more reliable than commercial ones.

106 Hatband
Hatbands are a great way to display your skills and silently tell others a little about yourself.

110 Reflector Oven
Warm meals and oven-baked goods in the wild are a lot easier with these handy ovens.

INTRODUCTION

As I worked on this new edition of *Building Outdoor Gear*, I started to realize just how long the book has actually been in the making. It really started in 1970 when I signed on as an Outdoor Resources instructor at the Skowhegan Regional Vocational Center in Maine. I would be teaching junior and senior high school students about outdoor Maine, but mostly it was expected to be a hands-on type of program. These students wanted to work with their hands! I started wracking my brain for outdoor-related projects that would grab the students' interest and inspire them to pursue outdoor careers. I was also a licensed Maine Guide, and now with my summers free I could build a guiding business of canoe trips on Maine's wilderness rivers. These two careers proved the ideal combination for developing and proving outdoor equipment, and that is just what I set out to do.

As I saw a need in my guiding business for better equipment, I worked with my students during the school year to develop it. Once in a while we hit it lucky and got it right the first time, but more often than not something unforeseen in the shop became evident on the canoe trail. In the fall we went back to the shop and made improvements. This evolution continued over the nearly 30 years I spent at the center. Some equipment ideas came from the students themselves, designed to fill their own needs. To that end I do not take credit for the actual invention of any of the projects—if invention is the correct word—but I can own up to making improvements on all of them. The laminated canoe paddle is an exception; it originated solely in my mind, and required a number of years of trial and error before it reached the stage you see here.

Outdoor people don't make their own gear to save money. Fly fisherman who tie their own flies or make their own rods will readily admit, if they are honest, that they have more money tied up in material and tool inventory than they would have ever spent on store-bought flies or fly rods. The same is true for hand-loaders who put together ammunition for hunting or target practice, or duck hunters who carve their own decoys. Economy isn't the objective; it is the satisfaction of making something and then seeing it do what it was designed to do. But, they will argue, what they make is better than what they can buy. I heartily agree, and these projects are a case in point.

I readily grasp anything that will improve what I make and use. When I became proficient with epoxy materials and related products, I realized that this was the most important technology for the do-it-yourself outdoor person since the birch bark canoe.

I realize this isn't the type of book most people will sit down and read from cover to cover, but do pay close attention to the chapter on epoxy before attempting to make anything using that material.

I consider it one of the safest materials I have worked with, but it is a combination of chemicals and should be treated with respect. Read about what I have learned and pay close attention to the manufacturer's directions before moving on with your project. Protective surgical-type gloves are readily available, and you should wear them when handling epoxy.

Epoxy is the all-important ingredient in my book *Building A Strip Canoe*. It is also the most daunting to first-time builders, and rightly so: it is expensive stuff, and no one wants to risk messing it up. Many of these projects give you a chance to try out the epoxy materials on a small scale and gain experience and confidence. When you discover how your projects stand up to water, weather, and hard use, you will be as sold on the material as I am. Then go ahead and build a canoe!

The laminated paddle illustrates three of the most important uses of epoxy. The ultimate in waterproof adhesives, epoxy glues together the wood parts.

A canoe party relaxes in an Allagash campsite. In spite of the fact that it rained most of the day, everyone is in good cheer, and it is obvious that they are comfortable.

Fiberglassing gives the blade strength, and liquid epoxy coats the shaft to waterproof it and protect it from the elements.

On weeklong river trips, we used our canoe chairs ashore more than in canoes. When they are in canoes, they make a comfortable place for a third person to ride or fish while some Good Samaritan paddles them around. Making a canoe

chair is a good way to learn several new skills. Curving the back of the chair requires some elementary wood bending. Joining the chair parts calls for mortise and tenon joints, the strongest in a woodworker's repertoire. Gluing uses epoxy. And finally, making the seat introduces caning. Cane is the most comfortable and lightweight material for outdoor sitting I have come across yet, and I highly recommend it. Three different projects in this book use caning. It isn't hard to do when you break it down step by step. An added benefit of learning this skill is you will be able to put new seats in those old chairs you have stored in the attic.

I included the caned canoe or boat seat project with comfort in mind. Anyone who has spent a day on a hard, unyielding, plastic or metal boat or canoe seat will readily agree that this seat is worth the time and effort to produce.

The third caning project is the wood pack frame. The caning is optional, but it does add comfort and class. I provide instructions for two wood-bending methods, and in making this frame you can try either. The frame project also appears in an earlier book of mine, *The Canoe Guide's Handbook,* and a number of people told me they bought that book just to make the pack frame or the trip boxes.

The trip boxes have brought me a lot a personal satisfaction. A year or so after publishing *The Canoe Guide's Handbook,* I started to see canoes going by with "my" boxes in them. Of course, I knew where they got the plans, so I had an opening to meet a lot of nice folks who would have otherwise paddled on by anonymously.

The boxes are not hard to make, but they do take time and are not for the one-time camper. But for those who intend to spend life in the outdoors, whatever the favorite activity, the boxes are a good investment in time and money. They will last most folks a lifetime. Mine saw constant use in my guiding business through the years and are still going strong, with only minor repairs along the way.

I have never owned a boat other than a canoe. While I thoroughly enjoy paddling with the peace and quiet and everything else that activity entails, there are times when a little motorized help is called for.

Some folks buy a square-stern canoe for this, but I prefer the side mount. It is more comfortable for me to control a side motor than one that is behind me, and it makes my canoe just that much more versatile.

Finding that the commercial, so-called "universal fit-all" mounts actually fit nothing, I decided to make my own. After several tries, each improving on the previous, I had a solid, easily attached and detached motor mount. I don't list exact dimensions and measurements for this project, because it is designed to be a custom job. Instead, I give directions to guide you in fitting your mount to your canoe.

I cannot count the number of times I have loaned my bucksaw to neighboring campers who thought all they needed to camp in the Maine woods was an ax—or, worse, a hatchet. I guess you could get your firewood with one of these tools, but you would probably soon decide the effort is not worth the results. Camp saws are available at outdoor stores and most of the discount stores that carry camping supplies. Any of them are better than just an ax, but none will do the job like a little camping bucksaw. I have included instructions for making two different bucksaws. I designed one, and a friend designed the other. Take your pick. They don't take up much space in your duffel and when they get dull, all you need to do is replace the blade.

Tips and Tidbits

I've accumulated some useful tips and recipes in my decades of outdoor experience. They don't all fit neatly together, so I've chosen to scatter them throughout the chapters wherever there was a bit of extra space. There's not always a correlation between the chapter and the tip.

For instance, a recipe for camp biscuits shows up on page 21, in the midst of a discussion about epoxy. Biscuits and epoxy are both good things, but they don't mix. So finish the epoxy and *then* make the biscuits.

Through the years, people repeatedly asked me where to buy reflector ovens. Good ones are hard to find, so I have provided three possibilities. Build your own from the instructions provided in this book, or buy from one of the two Maine outdoorsmen listed in "Resources and Supplies."

The personal hatband is a fun project that gives you a chance to show who you are and what you are about, but in a subdued and quiet way. Material and decoration possibilities abound. Let your imagination run wild!

Hints, tips, ideas, and recipes I have written about through the years in columns and articles are sprinkled here and there throughout the book. As with the major projects, I used them throughout my guiding career.

Early in my writing career I subscribed to a magazine for writers. In it I read an article on how to write how-to articles and books. The author said, "Don't tell them completely how to do anything. Leave an opening for follow-up articles." I found that advice disgusting and vowed I would either tell all I knew or nothing at all. That is what I have done in this book, and all my others. Previous editions of this book and my other books have been around long enough that I know I succeeded with them. I hope you find something here that will make your outdoor experiences a little better, and that you will find great pleasure and satisfaction in the process. However, if I have slipped up somewhere along the line, I assure you it was not so I could write a follow-up book. So let me know; I am available by phone, e-mail, or mail. My contact information is listed in "Resources and Supplies."

I will be pleased to hear from you, good or bad.

Gil Gilpatrick

Having a Compass Handy

Those who scoff at carrying a compass merely show their ignorance, not their prowess in the woods. For a variety of reasons, my friend Dick Mosher and I had each found ourselves in the woods without a compass from time to time. We didn't plan on it—it just happened. In a worst-case scenario not having a compass could lead to serious consequences, but even if you don't end up getting lost for an extended period, a compass makes things more convenient and often saves you a lot of time and effort in getting oriented again. Then Dick came up with this idea.

Just buy a small, good-quality compass and wear it around your neck, all the time. It will not be apparent under your shirt, but when you need it, it will be available quickly and reliably. Good quality, liquid-filled compasses can be purchased very reasonably; mine was designed to carry on a key ring.

Dot Gil's Barbecued Hot Dogs or Chicken

This isn't really one of those things you will want to prepare on the trail, so do it at home instead and freeze it to take along in the cooler. I include it because it has been so popular with my guests and reheating it in camp is really easy. Increase or decrease quantities according to your needs. I usually figure on 3 hot dogs or 1½ chicken breasts per person.

Frankfurters or chicken breasts
4 tablespoons of butter or margarine
2 cans of condensed tomato soup
½ cup of brown sugar
½ cup of water
3 tablespoons of vinegar
2 tablespoons of lemon juice
1 onion
½ cup of chopped green pepper

When we make these for home use we use a knife to score the hot dogs with a knife corkscrew-fashion and then brown them lightly in a skillet with butter. However, the rigors of freezing and reheating cause corkscrewed hot dogs to break up, so for trail use I forego that. Broil or grill the chicken breasts.

Mix the sauce ingredients and simmer in a covered pan for about 10 minutes. Then add the browned hot dogs or chicken and simmer for another 10 or 15 minutes. I like to serve them over hot cooked noodles, rice, or buns.

To prepare for trail use, bag cooled hot dogs or chicken and sauce, tie securely, and freeze. All you need to do on the trail is heat them, cook rice, and serve with a vegetable and biscuits.

Chapter 1

USING EPOXY

Clockwise from upper left are two brands of epoxy and related items I have used extensively: West System resin and hardener give the correct ratio with one pump of each. Raka requires two pumps of resin for every one of hardener. Cedar flour or sanding dust makes a great filler for nail holes or mistakes; buy it or save your own. Cotton fibers are used for epoxy glue, which can be thick to fill voids or thin as needed. Fiberglass cloth comes in a variety of weights.

Epoxy is the ingredient that many of the projects in this book have in common. The techniques of using epoxy are generally the same no matter what the final product is to be, so I will give a basic overview here instead of repeating it in the instructions for each project. When epoxy techniques stray from these basic instructions, I will provide more information in the project instructions.

Many of the projects in this book call for the use of epoxy resin, fiberglass, and other related materials. Epoxy opens up a whole new world to those interested in building quality outdoor equipment that will stand up to years of abuse, moisture, cold, and everything else Mother Nature can throw at it. It is exciting to use because it offers so many possibilities. As a waterproof glue, it is unsurpassed. As a resin for fiberglassing it provides wonderful adhesion to wood and other materials and remains flexible in all kinds of weather. Fillers, thickeners, and a variety of other products have also been designed for use with epoxy resin. Take some time to familiarize yourself with epoxy before attempting to use it.

I have used two manufacturers for my epoxy: West System by Gougeon Brothers, Inc. and Raka Inc. Both are listed in the supply sources in the appendix. I strongly recommend ordering *Gougeon's Technical Manual & Product Guide*. It provides a complete listing of Gougeon's extensive product line, gives information on using each of the products, and notes safety guidelines that apply to other epoxy brands as well. I extracted much of the following information from that publication, with some modifications based on my own experience with the projects. I also recommend asking to be put on the mailing list to receive the Gougeon publication called *Epoxyworks*. It comes out a couple of times a year and is filled with ideas from Gougeon's own shop and from people who have used epoxy to solve problems. Raka has a weekly e-newsletter that you can sign up for on their website.

Being Safe

In more than 30 years of using various fiberglassing products, I have tried quite a variety of materials. Many of them were extremely caustic, high-smelling, and just plain unpleasant to work with. When I first tried epoxy resin, I thought I had died and gone to canoe builder's heaven. The almost odorless and relatively safe material was a dream come true and because of the wonderful results I obtained with it, I have not been tempted to use anything else. However, as with any other chemical substances, epoxy products are not without certain hazards, and you cannot be too careful when handling them. Please follow the company's safety guidelines as well as your own old-fashioned common sense.

By themselves, resins rarely cause skin sensitization. Hardeners, however, are considered skin irritants and sensitizers—but their toxicity is greatly reduced when they are mixed in the proper ratio with the resin. Even so, you should take adequate handling precautions. Gougeon recommends strict observance of the following safeguards.

1. Avoid all direct skin contact with resin, hardeners, and mixed epoxy by wearing protective clothing.
Wear plastic gloves whenever you handle epoxy materials. Barrier skin creams provide additional protection. Use a waterless skin cleanser to clean uncured epoxy from the skin. Never use solvents to remove epoxy from your skin. Always wash thoroughly with soap and water immediately after skin contact with resin, hardeners, or solvents.

2. Protect your eyes from contact with resin, hardeners, mixed epoxy, and solvents by wearing safety glasses or goggles.
If contact occurs, immediately flush the eyes with liberal quantities of water under low pressure for 15 minutes. If discomfort persists, seek medical attention immediately.

3. Avoid inhaling vapors.
Use epoxy only in areas with good ventilation. In close quarters, such as boat interiors, be especially careful to exhaust the space and provide a supply of fresh air.

Wear a dust mask when you sand epoxy, taking extra care if it has cured for less than a week.

4. Stop using the product if you develop a skin rash while working with epoxy.
Resume work after the rash disappears, usually three or four days later. When you go back to work, improve your safety precautions and prevent any skin contact whatsoever with resin, hardeners, and mixed epoxy, as well as their vapors. If problems persist, consult a physician.

5. Do not operate power machinery or climb ladders if you have been working with solvents in a confined area.
If you feel tired, nauseated, high, or irritable while using solvents, move immediately to fresh air.

6. Clean up spills with a squeegee and paper towels.
Scrape up as much material as possible with a squeegee before using paper towels. Sand or clay-type absorbent material may be used to contain or soak up large spills. Clean residue with acetone, lacquer thinner, or waterless hand cleaner. Scraped-up resin or hardener that is uncontaminated may be strained for use.

7. Dispose of resin and hardener and empty containers safely.
Before disposing of resin and hardener containers, puncture corners of cans and drain residue into clean containers for reuse. Do not dispose of resin and hardener in a liquid state. Waste resin and hardener should be mixed and reacted to a non-hazardous solid before disposal. Place pots of mixed resin and hardener outside on the ground to avoid the danger of excessive heat, fumes, and possible fire. Dispose after reaction is complete and mixture has cooled. Follow federal, state, or local disposal regulations.

8. Keep resins, hardeners, fillers, and solvents out of reach of children.
For additional safety information and data, visit www.westsystem.com or www.raka.com. Click on "safety" or "MSDS" (Material Safety Data Sheet). It is a good idea to order or download the MSDS for the material you order and keep it on hand in your shop.

Handling Epoxy

Mixing the epoxy resin and hardener begins a chemical reaction that gradually changes the combined ingredients from a liquid to a solid. Careful measuring and thorough mixing are essential for the reaction to occur. Whether you apply the resin/hardener mixture as a coating or modify it with fillers or additives, observing the following procedures will assure a controlled and thorough chemical transition to a high-strength epoxy solid.

Dispensing

Most problems related to curing epoxy can be traced to the wrong ratio or resin and hardener. Follow the manufacturer's instructions to ensure you use the correct ratio of epoxy resin and hardener. I list the following as examples of materials I have worked with.

West System products are designed to be mixed at a five-to-one or three-to-one ratio. Inexpensive mini-pumps from West System make accurately measuring these ratios easy. The pumps are sold in pairs, and one full pump of resin for each one full pump of hardener results in the correct ratio. To measure a five-to-one ratio without pumps, make six equally spaced marks on a stick up to the desired level. Put the marked stick in the straight-walled container, such as a coffee can, and pour in resin up to the fifth mark. Then add the hardener up to mark six.

Raka products I used were designed to be mixed at a two-to-one ratio. Raka sells pumps that both dispense the same amount, so two pumps of resin for every one pump of hardener will result in the correct two-to-one ratio. Reaching that ratio without pumps is easier if you use a graduated container. For example, for 18 ounces of mixture, you would first measure 12 ounces of resin into the graduated container, then add hardener to bring the total up to the 18-ounce mark (it will take 6 ounces). You could also use the marked stick method here with three equally spaced marks.

Given the low cost of pumps from either manufacturer, buying them will make your epoxy experience a lot easier and more pleasant. In any case, do not attempt to control the cure time by altering the recommended epoxy-hardener ratio! The correct way to control cure time is by buying the appropriate hardener.

Mixing

Mixing epoxy with error-free results involves three separate steps.

1. Dispense the proper proportions of the resin and hardener into a mixing pot.
Begin with a small batch if you are unfamiliar with the pot life or coverage of the epoxy. You can always mix up a little more.

2. Stir the two ingredients together thoroughly with a wooden mixing stick—I recommend one to two minutes.
Scrape the sides and bottom of the pot as you mix. Use the flat end of the mixing stick to reach the inside corner of the pot.

3. Add fillers, additives, or pigments, if required, after thoroughly mixing resin and hardener.
If you are going to be using the mixture out of a roller pan, mix it thoroughly in a mixing pot before transferring it to the roller pan.

CAUTION: The chemical reaction that cures epoxy generates heat. A plastic cup full of mixed epoxy will generate enough heat to melt the cup, if left to stand for its full pot life. If a pot of mixed epoxy begins to exotherm (heat up), quickly move it outdoors. Avoid breathing the fumes. Do not dispose of the mixture until the reaction is complete and has cooled.

A couple of holes in the deck and a short length of shock cord (bungee cord) allow you to store your canoe line safely. This is especially important when running white water. It is nice to have the line out of the way any time it is not needed.

Storing Canoe Lines Safely

Canoe lines, or painters, are a necessity for any canoe traveler. They are useful for lining the canoe down through unrunnable rapids, towing it up through pitches too steep to pole, and loading or unloading a floating canoe. But these lines can become a danger if they become entangled in the paddler's legs during an upset in whitewater.

Safe storage with immediate availability is the answer. The best way I have found to do this uses a length of small diameter shock cord (bungee) (³⁄₁₆" or ¼" [5 or 6mm]). These cords are available from marine dealers. Drill two holes 5" or 6" (127 or 152mm) apart in the canoe's deck. Pull one end of the shock cord through one hole and knot it underneath. Pull the other end through the other hole and make another knot, pulling the cord so there is a little tension before tying off. Cut off the unused cord then repeat the process for the other end of the canoe. When you're not using the rope, loop it and tuck it safely under the shock cord.

Curing

The time it takes an epoxy mixture to change from a liquid to a solid is generally called "cure time." It has three phases: open or wet lay-up time (liquid state), initial cure time (gel state), and final cure time (solid state). The speed of the reaction and the length of these phases and the total cure time varies relative to the ambient temperature and mass of curing epoxy.

Open time: Open or wet lay-up describes the time the resin/hardener epoxy mixture remains in a liquid state and is easily workable or suitable for application. It occurs after thorough mixing, and the end of this phase marks the last opportunity to apply clamping pressure to a lay-up or assembly and obtain a dependable bond.

Initial cure phase: The open time is over when the mixture passes into an initial or partial cure phase (sometimes called the green stage) and reaches a gel state. At this point the epoxy feels tack-free, and you can still dent it with your thumbnail. It is hard enough to shape with files or planes, but too soft to dry-sand. Because the mixture is only partially cured, a new application of epoxy will still chemically link with it, so you can still bond or recoat the surface without sanding. This bit of knowledge can often save you a lot of work with the sander and possibly produce a superior product.

Final cure phase: In the final cure phase, the epoxy mixture has cured to a solid state and allows dry sanding and shaping. You should not be able to dent it with your thumbnail. The epoxy has reached about 90 percent of its ultimate strength, so you can remove the clamps. The epoxy will continue to cure over the next several days at room temperature. A new application of epoxy will not chemically link to it, so before recoating you must sand the surface of the epoxy to achieve a mechanical, secondary bond.

Controlling Cure Time

You may select a resin/hardener combination based on the length of its overall cure time or on its "pot life." Slow hardener gives you 20 to 25 minutes of pot life and nine to 12 hours to cure to a solid state. Fast hardener gives you nine to 12 minutes of pot life and six to eight hours to cure to a solid state. However, these times are only a guide, and they can be altered by variations in the quantity mixed, container shape, and temperature at which the material is used.

Quantity: Mixing resin and hardener creates an exothermic (heat-producing) reaction. The greater the quantity, the more heat generated, and the shorter the open time and overall cure time. Smaller batches of epoxy generate less heat then larger batches, providing longer open and overall cure times. A thicker joint or layer of epoxy cures faster than a thin layer.

Container shape: You can dissipate the heat a resin/hardener mixture generates by pouring the mixture into a container with greater surface area, such as a roller pan, thereby extending its open time. The epoxy cures faster while it's in the mixing pot, so the sooner after thorough mixing it is transferred or applied, the more useful open time is available for coating, lay-up, or assembly.

Temperature: Heat can be applied or removed from the epoxy to shorten or extend open and cure times. A hot air gun, hair dryer, or heat lamp can be used to warm the resin and hardener before mixing or after the epoxy is applied, reducing the cure time. However, heating epoxy that has not reached its initial cure lowers its viscosity, allowing the epoxy to more easily run or sag on vertical surfaces. In addition, if the material coated with epoxy is porous—soft wood or low-density core material—heating may cause it to "out-gas," with air expanding and passing from the material, forming bubbles in the epoxy coating. This can be a concern if you desire a clear finish. Never heat epoxy over 120°F (49°C).

Adding Fillers

When I reference epoxy or resin/hardener mixture, I mean the resin and hardener without any fillers or thickeners added. When I talk about thickened mixture, I mean the resin/hardener mixture with one of the various additives mixed in. The most common thickener used for the projects in this book is cotton fibers used to make waterproof glue. The beauty of epoxy is the wide choice of products to obtain the best material for any particular job, and that you can tailor the material to your exact needs.

Thickness: The amount of filler added determines the thickness of a mixture and what it can be used for. An unthickened resin/hardener mixture has the consistency of syrup and is used as-is for sealing wood surfaces, fiberglassing, and coating. A slightly thickened mixture has the consistency of catsup and is used for bonding large areas such as panels and for injecting with a syringe. A moderately thickened mixture has a consistency similar to mayonnaise and is used for general bonding, filleting, and hardware bonding. When thickened to the maximum, the mixture is like peanut butter and is used for filling gaps, filleting, bonding uneven surfaces where gap filling is require, and as fairing putty.

Mixing: Always add fillers in a two-step process. First mix the desired quantity of resin and hardener thoroughly before adding fillers. Begin with a small batch. Then stir in small amounts of the appropriate filler until the mixture reaches the desired consistency. Be sure all of the filler is thoroughly blended before you apply the mixture.

Preparing the Surface

Whether you are bonding, laminating, filleting, fairing, or applying fabrics, success depends on both the strength of the epoxy and how well the epoxy adheres to the surface. Unless you are bonding to partially cured epoxy, the strength of the bonds relies on the epoxy's ability to mechanically "key" into the surface. Epoxy has a remarkable ability to do this: that is why it is such an amazing and versatile material—and why the following steps of surface preparation are critical for any secondary bonding operation. Even if your project doesn't use secondary bonding, you will certainly find the concept useful for any equipment repairs you may need to do. I have used epoxy to repair everything from

Attaching Canoe Lines

Novice canoeists often overlook canoe lines, but experienced paddlers know how important they can be. Most canoes come equipped with some means of attaching a line, or painter, as purists like to call them. Usually it is just a hole in the deck through which a line can be passed and knotted in place. For the serious canoeist this spot is too high for either lining or towing, as it can make the canoe tip dangerously sideways in some situations.

To overcome this, you can equip almost any canoe with a low-level line attachment. All you need is a piece of ½" or ¾" (13 or 19mm) copper pipe and some epoxy with cotton fibers (I like the ¾" [19mm]).

Drill a hole large enough for the copper pipe through the ends of the canoe just above the waterline. Rough up and clean up the copper pipe with sandpaper to ensure a good bond with

This low line attachment works on almost any canoe, making it safer to line through rough stretches and easier to tow if that ever becomes necessary. just drill a hole near the waterline and then use epoxy to seal a short length of ¾" (19mm) copper pipe in place.

the epoxy. Seal the pipe in place with an epoxy-cotton fiber mixture. When it has cured, cut off the ends of the pipe flush with the canoe hull and smooth up and touch up around the work area. I have used this technique on strip canoes, ABS canoes, and fiberglass canoes, all with good results.

automobile gas tanks to my wife's sewing machine.

Cleaning: Surfaces to be epoxied must be free of any contaminants, including grease, oil, wax, and mold release. Clean contaminated surfaces with a silicone and wax remover, such as DuPont Prep-Sol™ 3919S. Acetone or lacquer thinner works well on many contaminants. Wipe the surface with plain white paper towels before the solvent dries. Clean surfaces before sanding to avoid sanding the contaminant into the surface.

CAUTION: Follow all safety precautions when working with solvents.

Removing Amine Blush: Special preparation may be required for epoxy surfaces. Amine blush, which can appear as a wax-like film on cured epoxy surfaces, is a byproduct of the epoxy curing process and may begin to form during the initial cure phase. The blush is water-soluble and can easily be removed, but also can clog sandpaper and inhibit subsequent bonding if not removed. To remove the blush, wash the surface with clean water and an abrasive pad. I recommend the 3-M Scotch-brite™ 7447 General Purpose Hand Pads. Dry the surface with plain white paper towels to remove the dissolved blush before it dries on the surface. The surface should appear dull. Sand any remaining glossy areas with 80-grit sandpaper. Wet-sanding the

surface also removes the amine blush. Non-blush hardeners are available and are all I use now.

Remember, epoxy surfaces that are not fully cured may be bonded to or coated with epoxy without washing or sanding. This means that standing by and applying the subsequent coating at the proper time can save you a lot of work, if you have the time to do that. If you plan to cover an epoxy surface with a coating other than epoxy—for instance, paint or polyurethane varnish with an ultraviolet filter—you must allow the epoxy to cure fully and then follow the sanding and cleaning procedures explained in the previous paragraph.

Drying: Bonding surfaces must be as dry as possible for good adhesion. If necessary, accelerate drying by warming the bonding surface with hot air guns, hair dryers or heat lamps. Use fans to move the air in confined or enclosed spaces. Watch for condensation when working outdoors or whenever the temperature of the work environment changes.

Sanding: Sand hardwoods and non-porous surfaces thoroughly to obtain an abraded surface. Aluminum oxide paper of 80-grit provides a good texture for epoxy to "key" into. Be sure the surface to be bonded is solid. Remove any flaking, chalking, blistering, or old coating before sanding. Remove all dust after sanding.

Gluing with Epoxy

I never cease to find new uses for epoxy glue. I call it glue, but it is actually resin/hardener mixture thickened with cotton fibers. There might be times when you would want to use some other thickener to make this glue, but I urge you to include cotton fibers in your first order: you will find a multitude of uses for it besides many of the projects in this book.

There are two types of bonding. Use single-step bonding when joints have minimal loads and excess absorption into porous surfaces is not a problem. Use two-step bonding for most situations because it promotes maximum epoxy penetration into the bonding surface and prevents resin-starved joints.

Two-Step Bonding

Before mixing epoxy, check all parts to be bonded for proper fit and surface preparation, gather all the clamps and tools necessary for the operation, and cover any areas that need protection from spills, drips, or whatever.

1. Apply straight (unthickened) resin/hardener mixture to both surfaces to be joined.
This is called "wetting out" the surface. Apply the resin/hardener mixture with a disposable brush for small or tight areas, or use a foam roller for larger areas. To wet out a large horizontal area, I recommend using a plastic squeegee to spread the mixture evenly over the surface. You may proceed with step two immediately or any time before the wet-out coat reaches final cure. In many cases, I like to wait until the wet-out layer gels so it will not dilute the thickened mixture used in step two. At other times, this is not important.

2. Modify the mixture by stirring in cotton fibers or other appropriate filler.
Make it thick enough to bridge any gaps between the mating surfaces and to prevent resin-starved joints. Apply an even coat of the thickened mixture to only one of the surfaces to be joined. Be sure to use enough so all gaps are filled and some of the material squeezes out when the parts are brought together.

Single-Step Bonding

In single-step bonding, you apply the thickened epoxy directly to both of the components without first wetting out with resin/hardener. When you use this method you should not thicken the mixture any more than necessary to bridge gaps in the joint, because the thinner the mixture, the more it penetrates the surface of the materials. Do not use this method for highly loaded joints or to bond end grain or other porous surfaces.

Clamping

You don't need a lot of clamping pressure. Very often just a staple or two is enough to hold things in position until the material cures. Use only enough clamping pressure to squeeze a small amount of epoxy mixture from the joint. This indicates the epoxy is making good contact with both mating surfaces. Don't use too much pressure—you don't want to squeeze all of the epoxy mixture out of the joint.

Anything you can find or devise to hold things in place will do, as long as the parts are held in place. Clamping possibilities include spring clamps, C-clamps, adjustable bar clamps, heavy rubber bands cut from inner tubes, nylon-reinforced packaging tape, weights, and vacuum bagging. When placing clamps near epoxy-covered areas, use polyethylene plastic or wax paper under the clamps so they don't inadvertently bond to the surface. Staples, nails, or drywall screws often work where conventional clamps will not.

Shape or remove any excess adhesive that squeezes out of the joint as soon as the joint is secured with clamps. Failure to do this now results in a lot of work later on. A wood mixing stick with one end sanded to a chisel edge is ideal for removing excess material.

Fiberglassing

Woven fiberglass cloth may be applied by either of two methods to provide reinforcement or abrasion resistance. It is usually applied after fairing and shaping are completed, before the final coating operation. The dry method involves applying the cloth over a dry surface, either before the surface has been wet out or after the wet-out coat has reached its initial cure (or final cure with sanding). I often call this wet-out coat sealer, because you are sealing the surface with resin to prepare it for the fiberglassing to come. The wet method involves applying the cloth to an epoxy-coated surface before the coat reaches its initial cure. Often the cloth is applied after the wet-out coat becomes tacky, which helps it cling to vertical or overhead surfaces. Because the wet method makes it more difficult to position the cloth, I prefer to use the dry method whenever possible. The dry method works for all the projects in this book.

No matter how big the fiberglassing job you face, mix your epoxy in small batches so you can work at a comfortable pace. Remember that your open time increases greatly once you start spreading the resin/hardener mix, so there is no need to hurry and risk spoiling your project.

1. Prepare the surface.
Because you will be fiberglassing over wood, this consists of sanding and making sure all surfaces are fair so the fiberglass cloth lies flat, without bubbles or air pockets.

2. Seal the surface by covering it with a liberal coating of resin/hardener.

3. If you can continue when the sealer coat has gelled (initial cure phase), go to step 5.

4. If you allowed the sealer coat to reach the final cure phase, sand the surface thoroughly to ensure a good mechanical bond for the next step.
Be careful not to sand through to the bare wood.

5. Position the cloth over the surface and cut it about two inches larger on all sides.
If the surface area you are covering is larger than the cloth size, allow multiple pieces to overlap by approximately 2" (51mm). On sloped or vertical surfaces, you may need to hold the cloth in place with several pieces of masking tape or staples until the resin has been applied.

6. Mix a small quantity of resin.

7. Pour a small pool of resin/hardener near the center of the cloth.

Camp Biscuits

All you need for these is a biscuit mix. You can make your own or take along a ready-made one from the grocery store. Four cups of the mix will yield 24 biscuits. Carry along pre-measured dry ingredients according to your needs for each meal.

Add the water until the dough is quite stiff and not at all runny. Drop the biscuits by the spoonful on the baking sheet and bake in the reflector.

Drop biscuits are a lot easier to make than the roll-out variety and they taste just as good.

Biscuit mix has many uses in camp, so look through the recipes and use your imagination. Take along a little more than you think necessary in case a new opportunity comes along.

8. Spread the epoxy over the cloth surface with a plastic squeegee, working the epoxy gently from the pool into the dry areas.

When the cloth has absorbed enough epoxy, it becomes transparent. If you are applying the cloth over a porous surface, be sure to leave enough epoxy to be absorbed by both the cloth and the surface below it. (If you sealed it properly, this is not necessary; see step 2.) Dry areas will show up whiter and less transparent than a properly moistened area. Try to limit the amount of squeegeeing you do. The more you work the wet surface, the more minute air bubbles are placed in suspension in the epoxy. This is especially important if you plan to use a clear finish. A roller or brush works well for applying epoxy to a horizontal surface, and is essential for applying cloth to large vertical surfaces.

9. Continue pouring and spreading (or rolling) small batches of epoxy away from the center of the cloth toward the outside edges, smoothing wrinkles and positioning the cloth as you go.

Check for dry areas and re-wet them as necessary before proceeding to the next step. If you have to cut a pleat or notch in the cloth to lay it flat on a compound curve or corner, make the cut with a pair of sharp scissors and overlap the edges for now.

10. Squeegee away excess epoxy before the first batch begins to gel.

Drag the squeegee over the fabric, using even-pressured, overlapping strokes. The object is to remove excess epoxy that would allow the cloth to float off the surface and avoid creating dry spots by squeegeeing too hard. Excess epoxy appears as a shiny area, while a properly moistened surface appears evenly transparent, with a smooth cloth texture. It could be labeled a satin finish. Later coats of epoxy finish filling the weave of the cloth.

Tying On a Sleeping Bag

If you carry your personal gear in a pack frame with a compartmented bag, this tip will make tying on your sleeping bag a little easier and a little more secure. Typically people tie the sleeping bag to the frame beneath the pack. That works well, but tying the sleeping bag on so it will not work loose requires considerable time and effort.

My solution is a combination of small rope and small shock cord. Actually, the shock cords I use are sold in camping supply stores as tent line tighteners. They are loops of shock cord with a wire hook. The line tighteners work equally well to tighten the sleeping bag tie-on line. Secure two shock cords to the top on the area where the bag is to go. On the bottom of the area, in positions corresponding to the shock cords, tie on lengths of nylon or other type of cord. To use, simply slip the nylon rope through the shock cord, pull it tight, and secure with a simple knot. It's quick, and the elastic cord holds the sleeping bag securely in place in all conditions.

11. Trim the excess and overlapped cloth after the epoxy has reached its initial cure, if possible.

The cloth cuts easily with a sharp utility knife.

12. Coat the surface to fill the weave of the cloth before the epoxy reaches its final cure stage.

Apply as many coats as needed to do this. Remember, if you must apply these coatings over the surface after it has reached the final cure phase, you must sand thoroughly and follow the instructions on removing amine blush.

In places where overlaps are made, such as where you make a corner, feather out the edges so you do not feel a ridge as you run your finger over it. This feathering is easily done with 80-grit sandpaper. When finished, apply one more coating of resin/hardener to complete the joint. After the final coating of epoxy, sand the entire project thoroughly to prepare it for a coating of paint or polyurethane varnish containing a UV filter. Before applying polyurethane or paint over a cured epoxy surface, be sure to thoroughly wash the surface with a liberal amount of water to remove all of the sanding dust. You may get a poor cure of the polyurethane or paint if you fail to do this.

If there is an end to the things that can be built and repaired with epoxy products, I have yet to reach it. Gougeon publishes a booklet listing some of the other uses of epoxy. It is worth looking at, but even more important for you is the things that you find to use it for. Give it a try; you won't be sorry.

Canoe Country Bread

Browsing a 100-year-old camping book one day, I came across a recipe for bread. It turned out to be the best bread I have found for day-in, day-out use on any outdoor expedition and, as it was simply called "bread," I took the liberty of naming it. You can bake it in a reflector oven, stovetop oven, or whatever you have. One loaf with cheese, peanut butter, etc., takes care of six people for lunch. All kinds of variations are possible. Add raisins or other dried fruit, streak in some cinnamon-sugar mix, and you have a tasty coffee cake.

I take the dry ingredients premixed and, when I'm ready to make it, simply add water, mix, and bake.

4 cups of flour
4 teaspoons of baking powder
3 teaspoons of salt
½ cup of sugar
2½ cups of water

After mixing the dry ingredients, add the water and beat the devil out of the batter for half a minute or so. Pour into a greased or oiled 9" x 9" (229 x 229mm) pan or equivalent, and bake for 50 minutes at 350 degrees. In actual use on the trail the time and temperature don't mean much; you'll know it's done when a stick inserted in it comes out clean. Using a shallow 9" x 9" (229mm x 229mm) pan instead of a loaf pan cuts down on the baking time—and the pan tends to be more versatile than a loaf pan.

Caning supplies. At the top is a jar of petroleum jelly. The hammer has limited use, but you will need it eventually. The purpose of the knife is obvious. Make from dowels, or buy, a good supply (at least a dozen) of hardwood pegs. Your cane may look different, but the large roll is medium cane and the small bundle is binder cane.

Chapter 2

CANING

Years ago, in an adult canoe building class, one of my students who had experience caning chair seats with natural cane remarked that he was going to do his canoe seats with the real thing. I asked him why. He replied that he liked the idea of using traditional materials, the modern plastic seeming somehow out of place. I laughed and pointed out that he was using space-age materials to build his canoe, even though the finished product did have a natural appearance. He laughed along with me and replied that he had not thought of it in that way. Since the students caned their seats at home, I never learned which he ended up using.

Natural cane has one disadvantage that makes it unsuitable for canoe seats, in my opinion. It stretches and sags in damp weather, and then it does not return to its original shape when dry. The plastic cane always remains taut and flexible, bounces back from the roughest treatment, and seems to be unaffected by heat and cold. I have plastic caned canoe seats that have been in use for so long, I'm

beginning to think the cane will outlast the wooden frame it is strung upon.

If you have prepared for the caning operation, you should already have the necessary tools and materials to complete this important phase of the seat project. The photo above shows the items you will need for weaving plastic cane, and I will explain the purpose of each item as we get to it. From time to time cane comes in different-looking spools and hanks, so yours might differ from the cane and binder in the photo. Vaseline is shown for a lubricating agent for the cane when you pull it through. The friction of the cane sliding between layers of cane can melt the plastic, so lubrication is necessary. I included the Vaseline because that is what the "experts" recommend. I personally just dip my fingers into a container of water and coat the cane with it before pulling through. It works fine, and I never had a melted cane! The Vaseline picks up a lot of dirt as you work—the water is a lot less messy.

1. Clamp the seat.

Get comfortable, and we'll get to work. I will be referring to the back and front of the seat from time to time, so let's establish which is which for our purposes. We will consider the wide part of the seat (closest to you) the front, and the narrow part the back. The two angled pieces in the photos will be called the sides. If your seat is of a different design, just establish the front from the back and be consistent. Some work with the seat in their lap, but I prefer to have it sturdily clamped in place at a convenient working height. Work out whatever works best for you.

2. Measure the cane.

Start out by counting the holes in the front and back to find the center hole of each, which you then mark with a peg. Get out a convenient length of cane. Somewhere around 12' (3,600 mm) works well. Use your arms as a convenient measure. Most people can reach roughly their own height with their arms outstretched.

Clamp the seat. Clamping the seat to the edge of a bench or table is a good way to secure it for caning. Free access to the top and bottom of the seat is necessary for efficient caning.

Insert pegs into holes as you go in order to keep the cane tight.

3. String up and down.

Start in the rear center hole and string the cane across to the front center hole. Notice that the cane has a right side and a wrong side. The rounded side should be up; you will have to keep it that way throughout the project. Be sure to leave 4 or 5" (102 to 127mm) of cane hanging below the seat wherever there is an end so that you will have something to get ahold of when you tie off later. You will go down through the front center hole and come up through the one to its right. Go across toward the rear and go down through the hole to the right of the rear center hole. Continue stringing the cane this way until the side is filled like photo 3 on page 25. Follow along with a peg from hole to hole to hold the cane tight as you work. You don't have to pull the cane really tight, but just enough to keep the strands straight and in place. Things will tighten up later when you begin to weave.

When you approach the angled sides, just keep the shorter strands parallel with the others by moving from hole to hole along the angled pieces. The shorter strands on each side may have to be pegged on both ends so that the cane will not be strung across the holes underneath the seat. When you have filled in the right side of the seat, string up the other side in the same manner.

4. String horizontally.

Start this step by pegging off the end of your strand in the hole next to the right rear corner. Go across the seat horizontally to the corresponding hole on the other side. You are stringing these strands right over those put on in the previous step. Continue stringing horizontally across your seat until it is filled from rear to front. Don't worry about all those untied strands hanging below the seat; we'll get to them shortly.

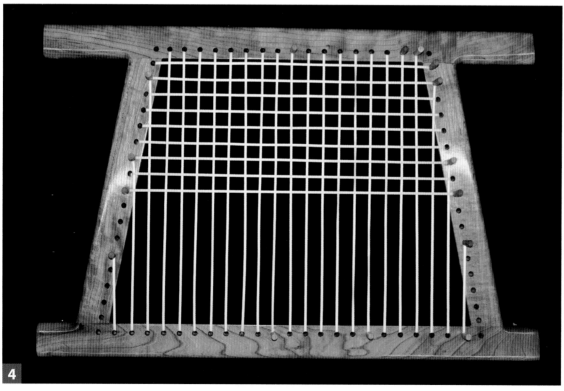

String horizontally. Continue stringing horizontally across your seat until it is filled from rear to front.

5. String up and down again.

So far, things are easy. They aren't going to get much more complicated either. This step is a repetition of Step 3. Start in a hole on one side or the other of the one you started in with Step 3, and string a new vertical layer of cane right over the layers put on in Steps 3 and 4. You'll end up with three layers of cane. The photo shows the right side of the seat with this step completed. I tried to push the strands apart a little so you could see the three layers.

6. Tie off the loose ends.

There are now a lot of pegs in the holes. Since they have to be removed and replaced when doing succeeding steps, it is a good idea to minimize them whenever possible. When your seat looks like this one, turn it over, and we'll do something about some of those loose ends and also get rid of some of the pegs at the same time.

This is the simple method of tying off the loose ends. It doesn't look too secure, but don't worry—the ties will stay in place. At the present time, you can only tie off the ends that have a loop next to them; those that don't are left until later. Take a look at the photo below for a visual on tying the knots. You want to thread the cane under the closest loop and then through the loop that creates.

I think neatness counts here. You may have noticed that the difference between professional and amateur work in any field is usually how the parts are finished that do not normally show. Your first seat can look like a pro's if you take a little care in tying off. Keep the ends all pointing in the same direction and cut them all the same length. I think it looks best if the ends are pointing in and are cut off at ⅛" (3mm) from the inside edge. You can remove all the pegs where you managed to tie off; leave the rest until you have a loop to tie them to. From now on, tie off what you can after completing each step.

5a

String up and down again. String a new vertical layer of cane right over the layers put on in Steps 3 and 4.

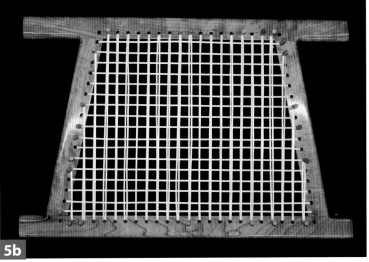

5b

Complete the new vertical layer.

6

Tie-off the loose ends. Don't be deceived—this tying-off method doesn't look too secure, but it works.

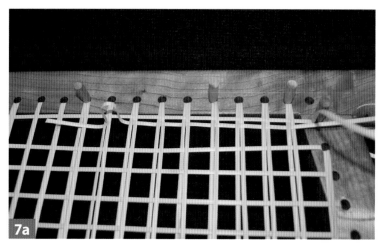

7a

Weave over the top canes and under the bottom canes.

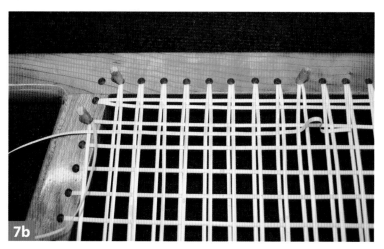

7b

Keep weaving. This photo shows that when you reach the left side and start back across, the weaving pattern looks identical to that of the first strand.

Complete the horizontal weave. Notice how the woven squares form a larger square hole in the woven pattern now that Step 7 is complete.

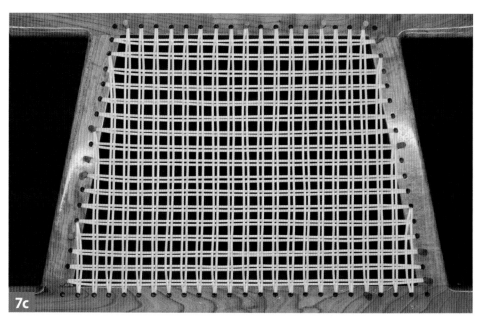

7c

7. Begin weaving.

Now you start weaving for the first time. You start this step in the same hole as you used to begin Step 4. Study the photo carefully. You will weave over the top canes and under the bottom canes, in that order. It is important that you keep the cane right side up, because if it twists as you pull it through, you'll probably have to take it out to straighten the strand. There isn't too much friction at this stage of the weaving, but it is a good idea to start lubricating the strands before you pull them through. Use water or petroleum jelly. You can weave all the way across before pulling the rest of the cane through if it is properly lubricated. Go down through the hole corresponding to the one you started with. Push the woven squares tightly together as you complete a strand. If you, like me, keep yourself weaving correctly when going from right to left by repeating, "over the top, under the bottom," then when you start going from left to right, reverse the phrase and say: "under the bottom, over the top." Same weave, different order.

Be conscientious about keeping the under-and-over weave consistent; it will prevent confusion and a lot of pulling out when you make the diagonal weaves in the following steps. Notice how the woven squares are pulled together and how they form a larger square hole in the woven pattern (see photo at bottom). Tie off wherever you can and you are ready to proceed to the diagonal weaving.

8. Weave diagonally from right to left.

Now the fun begins—making the diagonal weaves that complete the pattern. The first diagonal starts in the right rear corner and weaves under the pairs running from side to side and over the pairs running from front to rear. The photo at right shows the beginning of this step.

If you happened to reverse things in Step 7 (went under where you should have gone over, etc.) you can save pulling it all out by reversing this step and Step 9. Give the cane a little tug at the end of the weave just to ensure a good tight weave.

As you do your diagonal weaving, you will find that it is necessary to either skip a hole in the frame or to double up on one from time to time to preserve the spacing of the weave. Look closely at the photo at bottom and you will see where I doubled up on the side and skipped on the front. Also, notice that there are two canes coming from both corner holes. In the trade this is called a "Bird's Head," and it makes your job look really professional. Tie off where you can and move on to Step 9. Don't worry about tying off the corner holes. Leave the pegs there; we'll finish up the corners a little later.

Weave diagonally from right to left. The first diagonal starts in the right rear corner.

Keep the diagonal weave straight. This photo shows how to ensure you have your weave right. The peg points to where the diagonal can easily slip between the horizontal and vertical canes. If you have it wrong, the diagonal will take on a snake-like look instead of being straight like the ones in this photo.

Double up when needed. Look close to see where I doubled up some diagonal weaving on the side and skipped some on the front. Sometimes it is necessary to do this to maintain the spacing of the weave.

Weave diagonally from left to right. Weave over the pairs running from side to side and under the pairs running from front to rear.

The weaving is complete. Notice a nice "Bird's Head" in each corner. A close inspection will show those places where the cane was doubled up in a hole or a hole was skipped.

Packing Water Pails

If you cook for more than a few people, you probably have found that your cook set is barely large enough and there aren't enough water containers. Regular-size pails are bulky and are hard to stow away when not needed.

The best camping pails I have found are the plastic paint pails available for a small price wherever paint is sold. You can nest together as many as you think you will need, and they are small and flexible enough to pack away with other kitchen items, especially if you store something smaller in them.

9. Weave diagonally from left to right.

This step starts in the left rear corner and makes just the opposite diagonal weave of the sequence in Step 8. You will weave over the pairs running from side to side and under the pairs running from front to rear. It is increasingly important that you keep the canes lubricated as you pull them through, because the weave is getting tighter and tighter. If using water, keep your fingers wet as you pull the cane through them. About now you may be having a little trouble getting the cane up and down through the holes as they fill up with cane. There's plenty of room—you just have to push things around a little to open up the hole. Use a nail, an awl, or something similar to do this.

You can see in the photo at bottom left that there are now "Bird's Heads" in each corner. There are also a few skipped and doubled-up holes—but the important thing is to keep the cane running as straight as possible. When it is necessary to have the cane "lean" in one direction (because going straight there is no hole), make them lean as these in the photo do. It makes a better-looking job.

10. Cut the binder.

This step is called the binder, and is the finishing touch to your caning job. The binder cane is sometimes included with the medium cane, and sometimes you have to order it separately. Be sure to get it one way or another. The binder is wider than the weaving cane and its purpose is to cover up the holes around the edge of your seat. If, for some reason, you failed to get wide binder cane, then go ahead and use the medium cane; it is better than no binder at all.

Start by cutting a length of binder cane a couple of inches longer than the distance between the corner holes on the side you are starting first. Pull it tight and peg both ends into the corners.

11. Apply the binder.

With a piece of medium cane about 3' (1,000 mm) long, go up and down through the hole nearest one corner, around the binder. Leave enough hanging below to tie off later. Snug the medium cane down over the binder cane as shown in the photo. Move on and go up and down through the next hole. Repeat this until you use up the medium cane. Cut a new piece and continue until you have been all the way around the seat. When you have completed the binding, you should be able to tie off all loose ends hanging below the seat except the corners.

12. Drive in softwood pegs.

You should have a peg in each corner. If the pegs are made of hardwood (remember that most dowels are hardwood), replace them with pegs made of a soft wood such as cedar. You are finally going to use that hammer. Drive the softwood pegs securely into the holes, score them with a knife even with the seat surface, and break them off. If a little roughness persists, tap it with the hammer to smooth it out.

Any cane hanging below the lower surface of the seat at the corners can be trimmed flush with the surface. The seat is now complete!

11

Apply the binder. This is the finishing touch that covers the holes around the border.

12

The seat is complete!

Chapter 3

CANOE OR BOAT SEAT

In his book *Maine Lingo*, Maine humorist John Gould gives the following regional interpretation of an otherwise common English word:

Ample – Favored Maine word to express satisfaction at the table:

"Have more potatoes, Cyrus?"

"No thanks Helen, ample of everything."

A time-tested dialogue as old as Maine is between a deaf hostess and her gentleman guest. She speaks first:

More vegetables, Jonathan?

No, thanks—great sufficiency.

Been a-fishin'?

No, I say—I've got plenty!

Caught twenty?

No, no—I'm full!

Broke your pole?

No, no, ample, ample!

Small sample—pass up your plate!

In my section of Maine the word was also used, especially by my grandparents' generation, to describe something as being large enough that its size could be put out of mind for once and for all. My grandparents might be heard to say:

"That crock big enough, Ben?"

"Ample, Gertie, ample."

The reason for this bit of northern New England humor is simply so that you will know what I mean when I describe my canoe seats as ample. They are big enough so a person can spend the day on one of them and have room to squirm, wiggle, and shift to stay comfortable. Furthermore, the plastic cane has enough stretch and ventilation to make the above contortions all but unnecessary. Never, after a day on the canoe, did I feel the urge to stand and rub my posterior to restore circulation. Because most of my summer days were spent in the seat of a canoe, I valued this bit of comfort, and so I do not skimp on the seats. It takes only a little extra care to make a first-class seat. I can't for the life of me understand why some canoe builders insist on putting in seats that are little better to sit on than a thwart!

Making the Frames

The hardwood for the seats can be ¾" (19mm) or thicker. If you think you need a stronger seat for whatever reason, the additional material can come from the additional thickness or from additional width of your hardwood stock. Do whichever is easier for you with the tools and material you have to work with. I have found ¾" x 1½" (19 x 38mm) material to be adequate for most uses. If you need to beef up your seat either with thickness or width, you can make the adjustments to the instructions as needed. The instructions in this chapter will be based on material sawn to ¾" x 1½" (19 x 38mm). As for the kind of hardwood, as long as it is one of the stronger ones, like ash, oak, maple, cherry, or birch, the seats will be strong enough.

Materials
- Hardwood stock, ¾" x 1½" (19 x 38mm), 15' long (4,000mm)
- Epoxy and cotton fibers for glue
- Sandpaper, 80 and 120 grits
- Polyurethane
- Medium cane, 1 roll or hank with binder
- Carriage bolts, ¼" (6mm); two 6" (152mm), six 4" (102mm) with nuts and washers
- Dowels or scrap hardwood to make spacers for installing seats
- Petroleum jelly (optional)

Tools
- Table saw
- Power drill/driver
- Power sander
- Level
- Rule
- Handsaw
- 5/16" (8mm) drill bit
- ½" or 5/8" (13mm or 16mm) drill bit
- Hammer
- Knife
- Awl or nail
- 12 (or more) pegs for caning

1. Cut the hardwood for the seats.

Rip up enough hardwood stock to make the front, back, and sides of your seats. The front and back will have to be long enough to reach from gunwale to gunwale at the point in your canoe or boat where you will mount it. The sides will need to be 13 5/16" (338mm) when finished. For now, cut all four pieces to length plus about 1" (25mm) longer than finished length. The front and back of the bow seat should be 32" and 36" (813 and 914mm). For the stern seat, make them 17" and 21" (432 and 533mm). The front and back will be oversized; you cut to final length when the seat is installed in the canoe.

2. Mark the tenons.

Take a look at **Figure 3-1**, and you will see that the seat sides need to be cut at an angle of 12°, and the overall length of the pieces should be 13 5/16" (338mm). Make these measurements and cuts carefully, as they determine the angle of entry of your tenons into the mortises, which you will cut in the front and back pieces. The tenon length will be ½" (13mm), so measure from both ends back ½" (13mm) and mark for the tenon. You should make the tenon marks completely around the piece (top, bottom, and both edges)—that way you will have a guide to cut by no matter which way you turn the piece or how you make the cuts.

Covering a Pack in Wet Weather

During rainy weather in camp, space under cover is extremely limited. It usually consists of the tent or tents and a tarpaulin covering the eating area. Knowing this, I have tried to design my gear so it can remain out in the rain instead of competing with people for dry space. I haven't come up with a good way to make my pack waterproof—but I have found carrying a plastic garbage bag to pull down over the entire pack provides complete protection from rain or heavy dew. That enables me to leave my pack outside the cramped tent space, leaned against a tree, where it becomes my bureau away from home.

The plastic bag is also handy if an unexpected shower comes up during the day's travel. When I don't need it, I just stow the bag in my pack.

3. Mark the mortises.

Following the dimensions in **Figure 3-1,** mark the locations of the mortises in the front and back pieces. These mortises should each be made 1⅜" (35mm) long, or ⅛" (3mm) shorter than the width of the pieces being joined. See also the tenon detail. By making the joint slightly smaller than the parts, there will be no evidence of the joint on the finished seat. Or, to put it another way, you won't be able to see the ends of the mortises.

The mortise and tenon joint is the strongest wood joint in the woodworker's repertoire. So, combine this joint with epoxy glue and you have an unbeatable combination. Of course, you should always strive for a good wood to wood fit whenever you make a joint, but if you should make a mistake, the gap filling properties of the cotton fiber/epoxy mix will bail you out and save a lot of wood in the process.

4. Cut the tenons.

Carefully cut the tenons with a back-saw or other fine-toothed saw. A jig can be constructed to hold the parts at the correct angle, allowing you to make your cuts on a band saw, but for a few cuts it is hardly worth the effort. The tenons can be made on a table saw with the miter set at the proper angle and the blade at the proper height.

Notice in the detail of **Figure 3-1** that the tenon is cut 1/16" (2mm) smaller than the side of the seat. Also, the long side is trimmed so as to enter a vertically cut mortise. This trimming is unnecessary if you wish to cut the mortise at the proper angle, but usually it is easier to make it at a right angle to the surface, especially if you do it with power equipment.

5. Cut the mortises.

The simplest way to cut the mortises is with a ¼" (6mm) wood chisel and a hammer. If you have a power hand drill, you can save time by drilling inside your lines and then cleaning out what remains with the chisel. If you have a drill press, the whole job can be done on it with a 5/16" (8mm) router bit. The depth of the mortises should be a little deeper than the length of the tenons to ensure they will not bottom-out. Make them at least 9/16" (14mm) deep—⅝" (16mm) would even be OK.

6. Fit the joints together.

When both parts of the joints are cut, go ahead and fit them together. This will usually require some hand work with a fine rasp to make the tenon slide snugly into the mortise. If you made the mortises with a router bit on the drill press, the ends of the openings are rounded. It is easier to round off the ends of the tenons to match these openings than to square off the mortises. Either is OK, however.

7. Glue the joints.

When you are satisfied that all joints come together properly, glue them together with your epoxy glue. Put enough thickened mixture into the mortises that you are sure the cavity will be completely filled with the tenon and the glue. When the four joints are assembled, clamp together with bar clamps. Lacking bar clamps, a twisted rope between the front and back pieces will hold them firmly together until the final cure is reached. You may also be able to stand the seat on edge and place weight on top to hold things in place. At any rate, the joints should remain stationary until the final cure is reached (24 hours).

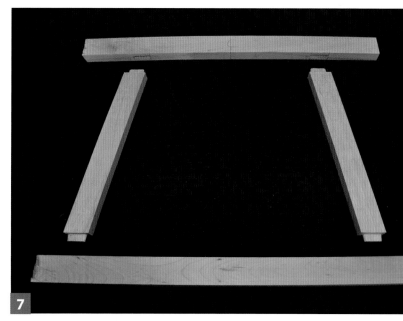

7

The seat parts ready to glue and clamp. With epoxy glue, it isn't necessary to exert a lot of clamping pressure, so a make-do method can be devised if bar clamps are not available.

8. Smooth the joints.

When the clamps are removed, you should smooth up the joints with a sander. Next, round off the outside of the seat either with a router and rounding cutter or by hand with a rasp, and then go ahead and do the rough sanding with 60 grit.

9. Locate the corner holes.

Before you do any further smoothing it is a good idea to mark and drill the holes for the caning. The completed holes can be seen in the photo below. The holes will be ¼" (6mm) in diameter and will be ¾" (19mm) apart on a line ⅜" (10mm) from the inside edge of the seat. The first thing to do is to measure out ⅜" (10mm) from the inside edge and draw a line on all four sides. Where these lines meet at the corners there will be a corner hole.

10. Mark the caning holes.

Next, find the center of each of the four sides and a mark it on the ⅜" (10mm) line. Now, measuring out toward the corners from that center mark, make a mark every ¾" (19mm) until you reach the corner. Since there will be a hole in each corner, you may have to fudge the last couple of marks before reaching the corner; they won't necessarily come out even. You can either make them a little closer than ¾" (19mm) or a little further apart, depending on the adjustment needed. The change of spacing will not be noticeable in the completed seat. Since you are starting from the center, whatever adjustment you make at one end of the side, you will make the same adjustment at the other. And, whatever adjustment you make on one side, you should do the same on the opposing side.

11. Drill the holes.

When you are satisfied with your marks, go ahead and drill the holes using a ¼" (6mm) drill bit. A drill press does the best job, but careful aligning with a power hand drill will do almost as well.

Rectangular Seat

You can make a very satisfactory seat by joining the parts at right angles rather than the angles of the seat sides in **Figure 3-1**. That seat was designed to follow the lines of the canoe gunwales, and looks good when installed. A strictly rectangular seat saves you the problem of careful cutting of angles and fitting them into the mortises. Tenons for rectangular seats can be easily cut with power equipment, whereas it is often easier to cut the angled tenons by hand than to set up power equipment for such a few cuts. If you decide on rectangular seats, then ignore the reference to angles in the following paragraphs and simply join yours at 90°.

12. Finish the wooden parts of the seat.

When the holes are all drilled, you can do the final sanding and coat your seat with polyurethane. Since you will probably do your caning with plastic cane (highly recommended for outside applications), which needs no finish, you will want the wooden parts completely finished before starting the caning process.

Now give the caning section a quick read and you will see that caning is not as scary as you may have thought.

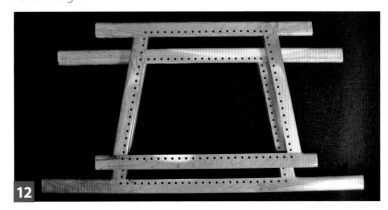

Finish the front and rear seats. Finish seats to be caned beforehand, because no finish is needed for the plastic cane. A couple of coats of exterior polyurethane bring out the color of these cherry wood seats.

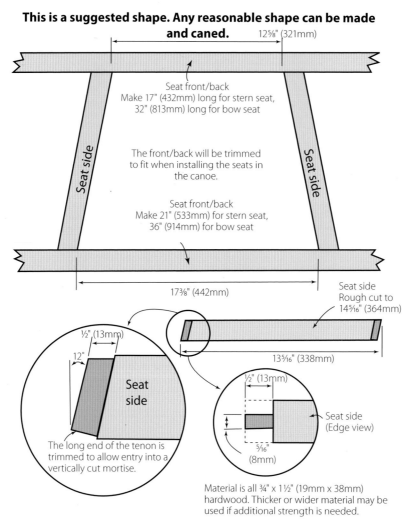

This is a suggested shape. Any reasonable shape can be made and caned. 12⅝" (321mm)

Seat front/back
Make 17" (432mm) long for stern seat,
32" (813mm) long for bow seat

The front/back will be trimmed
to fit when installing the seats in
the canoe.

Seat front/back
Make 21" (533mm) for stern seat,
36" (914mm) for bow seat

Seat side

Seat side

17⅜" (442mm)

Seat side
Rough cut to
14⁵⁄₁₆" (364mm)

½" (13mm)

12°

Seat
side

The long end of the tenon is
trimmed to allow entry into a
vertically cut mortise.

13⁵⁄₁₆" (338mm)

½" (13mm)

Seat side
(Edge view)

⁵⁄₁₆"
(8mm)

Material is all ¾" x 1½" (19mm x 38mm)
hardwood. Thicker or wider material may be
used if additional strength is needed.

Figure 3-1: Canoe seat dimensions. These are suggested dimensions for an "ample"
canoe seat. The mortise and tenon joint is the strongest wood joint in the woodworker's
repertoire. So, combine this joint with epoxy glue and you have an unbeatable
combination.

Other Joints

The mortise and tenon joint is not the only choice for assembling the seats, although it is my
preference and has stood the test of time on my canoes. A lap joint or doweled joint could be
used if you prefer.

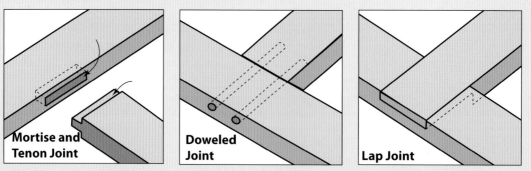

Mortise and Tenon Joint

Doweled Joint

Lap Joint

Other joints. There are a few wood joints that can be used to make seats. The one on left, mortise and tenon, is the strongest
and preferred. The doweled joint is easy to make, but its strength depends on the strength of the dowels. The lap joint is
probably the weakest, as you are cutting halfway through one of the members of the seat.

A tarp over the kitchen area is a good idea in fair weather or foul. On rainy days it is essential for keeping everyone dry as well as protecting the eating area and the fireplace. On sunny days it provides welcome shade.

Taking Tarps for the Kitchen Area

A good tarpaulin is an absolute necessity for an extended stay outdoors, because sooner or later it is going to rain. Spending an extended time in the confines of a small tent or under some makeshift cover and trying to prepare meals there is not fun at all. A tarp can provide cover for both people and the campfire—an important advantage whether you use the fire for meal preparation or just for the good cheer it seems to lend to long rainy days.

Some good-quality tarps are available for very reasonable prices, or you can make your own with a suitably sized piece of polyethylene. If you want to minimize weight and bulk, go for nylon tarps, which can be rolled up into surprisingly small packages.

Whatever kind of tarp you opt for, you will find it easier to handle in two pieces. I like to cover an area of about 12' x 18' or 20' (3,660 x 5,490 or 6,100mm), so I carry two nylon tarps that are each 10'x12' (3,050 x 3,600mm), overlapping them slightly when I put them up. Two smaller tarps are much easier to handle than one large one, especially if a small crew is available when you need cover in a hurry. If I need a quick shelter from a passing shower, I use just one.

A welcoming seat; after a long day of paddling, it feels good to lean back on one.

Chapter 4

CANOE CHAIR

Canoe chairs in Maine have a long history roughly paralleling that of the Registered Maine Guide. In Maine's early years, a canoe was a guide's most prized possession. It was, after all, the only means of transportation in Maine's northern wilderness. As other parts of the country became more civilized, the city folk started coming to Maine to enjoy its wilderness by hunting, fishing, camping, and just exploring.

Maine guides happily transported those folks into the wilds with their canoes. However, there was no way a guide wanted his guests to have any part of handling his precious canoe. In fact, he wanted passengers where they could do the least amount of damage given their inexperience in the woods and canoes. He wanted them as close to the bottom of the canoe as possible, and the only thing he wanted

Materials

- 2 board feet of hardwood (long enough for longest part—21" [533mm])
- (1) 2x4 x 8' (38 x 89 x 2,440mm) (common 2x4, for bending forms)
- 1 pair of 2" or 3" (51 or 76mm) strap hinges with screws
- 4 flathead machine screws with nuts, #6, 1 ¼" (32mm) long
- 1 pint of exterior polyurethane
- 1 hank of medium plastic cane
- Epoxy resin and hardener with thickener (cotton fibers) for glue
- Sandpaper: 1 sheet 80 grit, 1 sheet 120 or 150 grit

Tools

- Table saw
- Handsaw
- Carpenter's rule
- Protractor or other angle-measuring tool
- 4-in-1 rasp or fine wood rasp
- Drill press (optional)
- Electric hand drill (optional)
- Assorted small drill bits
- ¼" (6mm) chisel (for hand-cut mortises)
- Sander (optional)

Parts

All parts listed are of ash or other suitable hardwood except for the bending form, which can be made from a common 2 by 4.

- (A1) Back upper crosspiece (1) ⅜" x 3 ¼" x 18" (10 x 83 x 457mm)** (for hot bend)

or

- (A2) Back upper crosspiece (3) ⅛" x 3 ¼" x 18" (10 x 83 x 457mm)** (for glue-lam bend)
- (B) Back lower crosspiece (1) ¾" x 1 ½" x 16" (19 x 38 x 406mm)
- (C) Back uprights (2) ¾" x 1 ½" x 21" (19 x 38 x 533mm)
- (D) Seat sides (2) ¾" x 1 ½" x 18" (19 x 38 x 457 mm)*
- (E) Seat front and rear (2) ¾" x 1 ½" x 16" (19 x 38 x 406mm)
- (F) Skids (2) ¾" x ¾" x 20" (19 x 19 x 508mm)
- (G) Leg braces (2) ¾" x ¾" x 17 ½" (19 x 19 x 445mm)
- (H) Front legs (2) ¾" x ¾" x 5" (19 x 19 x 127mm)
- (I) Rear legs (2) ¾" x ¾" x 4 ½" (19 x 19 x 114mm)
- Bending form(s) (1) 2" x 4" x 8' (51 x 102 x 2,440mm) (spruce or whatever)
- 1 pair of 2" or 3" (51 or 76mm) strap hinges
- 6 flathead machine screws with nuts, #6, 1 ¼" (32mm) long

*Not exact finished length, to be trimmed for proper fit during assembly.

**To be cut out (see pattern) and bent over form(s).

Brittany Cost sits in a canoe chair waiting for the morning biscuits to bake. The chair can be used in the canoe or on shore, meeting my requirement that equipment do more than one job.

in their hands was a fly rod or rifle—definitely not a paddle! However, he had to give them some degree of comfort.

The canoe chair was the answer. It was low enough to ensure the occupant's weight was at the bottom of the canoe, and yet it raised the passenger's posterior so it didn't get wet from paddle drips, occasional leaks, etc. The chair also had a back, which allowed a degree of comfort most other seats found in or carried into the wilderness lacked.

Modern canoe travelers paddle their own canoes, usually in tandem with a companion. But the canoe chair still has a place in wilderness travel. Many times it is desirable to carry a third person in the canoe, perhaps a child or someone who cannot paddle. The chair is ideal for this, but its other uses also justify its presence on a trip. Ashore, it makes a comfortable seat—being able to sit down and lean back comfortably is a real treat after a hard day of paddling.

Many hardwoods are suitable for making a canoe chair. I usually use white ash because it is strong and abundant in Maine. I have also used birch and maple, and I have some black cherry on hand that I plan to try some time. All of the chair parts are small, so you could even build one with hardwood salvaged from old furniture, pallets, or shipping crates. However, avoid softer hardwoods such as basswood and poplar.

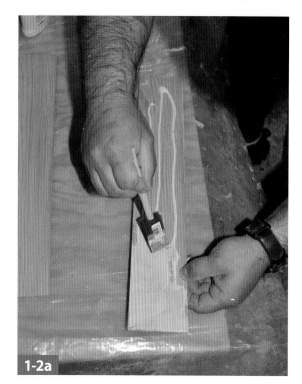

Glue the pieces.
Spread the glue evenly and cover the entire surface of the piece to be glued. Three ⅛" (3mm) pieces form a ⅜" (10mm)-thick back.

`1-2a`

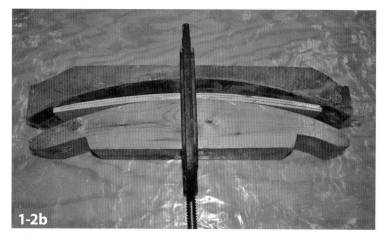

`1-2b`

As the parts are squeezed, they tend to slide out of alignment. Going slowly and keeping the pressure even helps prevent that.

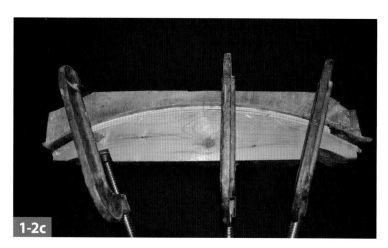

`1-2c`

Allow it to dry overnight.

Making a Chair

1. Form the crosspieces.
Start with the upper crosspiece (A), which requires special handling and drying time.

Option 1: Hot bend (A1).
This method requires one piece of ⅜" x 3¼" x 18" (10 x 83 x 457mm) hardwood to bend, and one piece of 2" x 4" x 8' (51 x 102 x 2,440mm) (spruce or whatever) to make the bending form.

Cut the hardwood to shape using **Figure 4-1.** Then use the other wood to make a bending form using the lower pattern in **Figure 4-2.** Put the piece to be bent into boiling water and leave it there for about an hour. (More is okay). It's nice to have someone to help you when you are ready to bend it over the form, but you can do it alone. Wear gloves to protect your hands. Remove the piece from the hot water and center it on the bending form. The hot wood is soft, so it is a good idea to protect it from the clamp jaws with a piece of scrap wood. Clamp one end and quickly bend the piece so you can clamp the other end. It will bend easily, but another pair of hands will come in handy to clamp it while you hold it in place. Let it dry for two or three days, then remove it from the form to sand and proceed with assembly. Don't dry it in a hot place such as beside a stove; a warm, dry place is best. If it is cool and damp, you may need to allow more drying time.

Option 2: Glue-lam (A2).
This method requires three pieces of ⅛" x 3¼" x 18" (10 x 83 x 457mm) hardwood to bend and one piece of 2" x 4" x 8' (51 x 102 x 2,440mm) spruce or the wood of your choice to make the bending form. Make the bending forms using both patterns in **Figure 4-2.** Then coat the ⅛" (3mm)-thick pieces of hardwood with glue on facing surfaces, stack them and, before the glue dries, squeeze them tightly between the upper and lower form. Use plastic tape or plastic to keep the pieces from gluing to the forms. Allow it to dry overnight, then cut it to shape using the pattern in **Figure 4-1.** The glue need not be absolutely waterproof, but should be water resistant. I have had good success with Water Resistant Titebond II Glue, a yellow glue

available at most hardware stores and home centers. Another option is Titebond III Glue, which is said to be completely waterproof. The glue plus the polyurethane finish is more than adequate insurance against delamination. Of course, you could use epoxy glue, but because this piece will not be used underwater, that would probably be overkill.

2. Cut the rest of the hardwood pieces.

While the back crosspiece dries, you have time to cut the rest of the hardwood pieces. This is easy on a table saw. Use the parts list as your guide. Once you have the stock dimensioned, cut all of it to the exact length given in the parts list. Note that the seat sides are a little too long: that is to allow for trimming during assembly, which I will address later. The upper crosspiece is also too long as cut from the pattern; you will trim that to length when you are ready to assemble the back.

3. Carefully mark the mortises and tenons.

Refer to **Figures 4-3** and **4-4.** This looks a little confusing on paper, with mortises going in different directions, but once you mark them you can hold the parts in their relative positions and all of the locations will make sense. If not, go back and check again. Note that the mortises to receive ¾" (19mm) stock are made ¾" (19mm) long. It is a good idea to make these mortises just a little shorter then ¾" (19mm). That way there is no danger of the mortise showing after assembly. Just cut the tenon down a little as you do the final fitting. The ones to receive 1½" (38mm) stock are 1" (25mm) long. The mortise to receive the curved upper crosspiece is cut at a 20° angle and is 1½" (38mm) long. Check the angle on your piece by following the instructions in the sidebar on page 55.

4. Cut the straight mortises.

With hand tools you can do them simply, using a chisel for the mortises and a fine-tooth saw for the tenons. If you choose that option, for the mortises it helps to drill away as much wood as possible before cutting away the rest with the chisel.

However, most people use power tools if they have them. I make the mortises with a 5⁄16" (8mm)

Cut the straight mortises. You can machine-cut mortises for the chair, as shown here, or do them by hand with a chisel.

Cut the angled mortises. You can cut the blocks at the necessary angle on a table saw and use a vise to hold them in place. If you don't have a drill press, simply clamp the three parts together. Holding the part at an angle is a good idea even for hand cutting—you can then hold the drill and chisel vertically.

spiral router bit in my drill press, holding the stock in place with a drill press vise. With a guide clamped to the drill press table and the depth set to 9⁄16" (14mm) (slightly deeper than the length of the tenons), you can complete most of the routing in a few minutes.

5. Cut the angled mortises in the curved upper crosspiece.

Cut the blocks at the angle you want for the mortises (20°). But you should check it on your own crosspieces in case there are variations. See the sidebar on page 55. However, if your drill press vise can be set at an angle, you don't need the angled blocks: simply set the vise at the proper angle and go ahead and rout. If you are cutting mortises by hand, it is still a good idea to put the piece in a vise at the proper angle, so you can hold the chisel vertically and know the angle is correct. Proceed very carefully when you do these angled mortises; it is very easy to get them angled the wrong way.

7

Adjust the mortises and tenons. This is a classic mortise and tenon joint, with the ends of the tenon rounded to fit into the machine-made mortise. Another option is to square off the ends of the mortise. Either works.

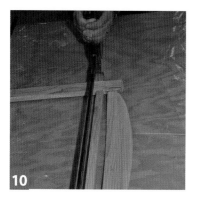

10

Glue and clamp the back. Use a temporary spacer to hold the uprights the same distance apart at the top as at the bottom. This keeps the clamping pressure from bending the crosspiece or pushing it too far into the mortise.

11

Glue and clamp the seat.

Assembling a Chair

7. Fit everything but the back together, adjusting the mortises and tenons as needed.

When all of the mortises and tenons are cut, you are ready for final fitting. Because I cut my mortises with a router bit, they are rounded on the end, so I have to either square the mortise ends or round off the tenons. I choose to round off the tenons, using a fine rasp for final fitting to their respective mortises. Save the back, with its angled mortises in the upper crosspiece, for last.

8. Adjust and fit the back.

Once all of the other joints are properly fitted, fit the lower crosspiece into the two back upright pieces. Lay the curved upper crosspiece next to the lower one and mark each end of the curved piece so it can enter the mortised back upright to a depth of ½" (13mm) on each side. Cut the curved piece to length by trimming each end. Then thin the ends of the curved piece to ⁵⁄₁₆" (8mm) so it can enter the ⁵⁄₁₆" (8mm) mortise. (See the detail in **Figure 4-4**.) The curved piece needs to enter the mortises far enough that the back uprights are parallel when the lower and upper crosspieces are in place. At this point, it is better to have it go a little too far than not far enough. When you glue up the back, place a spacer between the uprights, right below the curved piece, to prevent it from going in too far or bending under pressure from the clamp.

9. Sand all parts as needed.

Once all of the joints fit snugly together, take the pieces apart and sand each separately—it's a lot easier than when they are assembled. Then all you will need to sand later is around the joints you are about to glue up.

6. Cut the tenons.

Tenons are easily cut with a table saw, band saw, or radial arm saw. To use a band saw, mark each tenon on all sides so you will have lines to follow. To use a table or radial arm saw, be sure to set it up carefully for proper depth and with stops to control the length (½"—[13mm]). Once everything is set up, the cutting will go fairly fast. All tenons in this project are cut at 90° and are ½" (13mm) long. The tenons in the ¾" (19mm) stock are ¾" (19mm) wide, and the ones in the 1½" (38mm) stock are 1" (25mm) wide. The front and rear legs are different lengths to allow the seat to slope slightly to the rear. I have ignored the angle on the legs because it is so slight that it is impossible to tell whether the leg tenons were cut square or at the given angle when assembly is complete. I have tried it both ways. Now is a good time to round off the ends of the skids as shown in **Figure 4-6**.

10. Glue up the back.

Mix the epoxy and add enough thickener to get a thin paste. Single-step bonding will do the job as long as your mixture is rather thin. Coat both the mortise and tenon of each joint; hopefully the joints are good and tight, but if there are some gaps here and there, the epoxy does a great job of filling them. Use two clamps, with the upper positioned as shown in photo 10. When the clamps are in place, check that the uprights are square with the crosspieces. Be sure to remove all excess glue; it is a lot easier now than after it has cured.

11. Glue up the seat.

Glue up the seat the same way as the back, but without a spacer. Again, check for square and make adjustments if necessary before setting the parts aside to cure.

12. Remove clamps, sand joints, and round edges as desired.

Be sure the seat and back have cured completely before beginning this step. You will probably want to round off the front corners of the seat as shown in **Figure 4-5**. I like to round off the upper outer edge of the seat and the outer edge of the two back uprights with a router as well, but this is optional. Do not round off the bottom edge of the seat or the inside edge.

13. Lay out the caning holes.

Figure 4-5 shows how to lay out the seat. Start by making a line around the seat ⅜" (10mm) from the inside edge. This is the line of the holes, and where they cross at the corners marks the corner holes. Next, find the center of each side and mark it. Starting at the center mark, make a mark every ¾" (19mm) in each direction until you reach the corners. You will probably have to do some fudging with the last few holes, as it seldom works out perfectly. Make the marks a little closer together or farther apart as needed, but keep the spacing close to ¾" (19mm). Whatever fudging you do on one end (corner), do the same on the other end; whatever fudging you do on one side, do the same on the opposite side. You will probably end up with the same number of holes as shown in **Figure 4-5**, but if not, don't worry

Round the front corners. Tracing an object that has a pleasing arc is an easy way to round off the front corners of the chair. After cutting along the line, you can round over the top edge of the seat using a router or rasp and sandpaper.

Drill the caning holes.

about it. As long as the spacing is correct and holes on opposing sides line up, everything will be okay. The back is laid out in exactly the same manner as the seat, but remember that because of the curve, the upper crosspiece is a little longer than the lower crosspiece. Don't put in an extra hole as you approach the corner. Space the last three or four holes farther apart as needed, but keep the total number of holes the same as on the lower crosspiece.

14. Drill the caning holes with a ¼" (6mm) drill bit.

A drill press works best for this if you have one, but a power hand drill, or even a hand-powered drill, will do the job. When you are finished drilling, sand the surfaces as needed to clean up around the holes.

15. Assemble the skids, legs, and leg braces. Again, be sure to coat all surfaces with epoxy glue to ensure a good glue joint. When they have cured, remove the clamps and do any necessary sanding around the joints.

16. Give everything at least two coats of quality exterior polyurethane. Apply the first coat, let it dry thoroughly, and then sand lightly and remove the dust before applying the second coat. Be sure the second coat has dried thoroughly before you continue.

17. Cane the seat and back. Turn to page 24 for caning instructions. The caning for the seat and the back is done almost exactly as shown there. The exception is that, because all of the opposing sides on this chair are equal, you will not have to use the short pieces of cane as is shown in photo 3 on page 25.

Glue and clamp the legs, skids, and braces. After finishing all the machining on the seat, plan this step carefully. The parts must all be put together at once.

Apply polyurethane. I have had good luck with Zar brand.

Penobscot Cobbler

When fresh berries are in season you can do something a little more creative than just sit down and eat them off the bush. Want to really impress your companions on an outing? Try making this. This is a great way to use extra biscuit mix—and a reminder why you should always keep it handy.

4 cups of fruit or berries (any kind)

2 cups of biscuit mix

2 or 3 tablespoons of oleo (if available) or oil

Seasoning (pre-mix at home for just such an occasion)

1½ cups of sugar

2 tablespoons of cornstarch

½ teaspoon of cinnamon

¼ teaspoon of nutmeg

If no berries are in season and you still want to make a cobbler, take along dried fruit and rehydrate it.

Gently stir the fruit and the seasoning mix together in a large pan. I use the frying pan from my cook set.

Add a dollop of oleo to the biscuit mix and add just enough water to make a stiff dough. Spread and flatten the dough with your hands or a makeshift roller until it is the shape of the pan and a couple of inches larger in diameter. Place the flattened dough over the berries and tuck in the edges and seal them to the edge of the pan like a pie crust with your fingers.

Bake in a reflector for about 30 minutes. Usually when the crust is browned the cobbler is ready.

Cool before serving.

Finishing a Chair

18. Adjust the seat ends.

For comfort, the back should be at a 98° angle (or 8° from vertical) to the seat. See **Figure 4-6.** To achieve that, lay a straightedge against the bottom of the rear legs, use a protractor or similar tool to measure a 98° angle, mark it on the rear of both seat sides, then use a fine-tooth handsaw to cut along those lines. The back will rest against the bottom of the rear legs and against the angle cut you just made.

19. Attach the back to the seat.

Clamp the back in place and install two 2" or 3" (51 or 76mm) strap hinges. I prefer the 3" (76mm) because there is quite a lot of pressure when someone is leaning against the back, and the larger hinge holds up a little better. You can use wood screws to attach the part of the hinge that rests on the seat, but on the back, where there is more pressure, I like to drill holes and use at least a couple of #10 machine screws in each hinge. You may need to trim the skids or the ends of the sides of the back to make the chair stand up straight when in the stored, or upright, position.

That's it—the chair is finished! It folds down to 6" or 7" (152 or 178mm) high and stands on its own in the folded position.

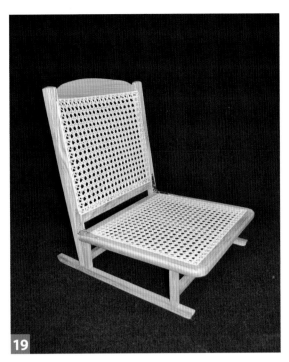

19

Attach the back to the seat.

The chair folds nicely for easy storage. If it doesn't stand up straight, you may need to trim the skids or the side extensions.

Make from ⅜″ x 3 ¼″ x 18″ (10 x 83 x 457mm) ash or other suitable hard wood.
Enlarge with 2″ (51mm) square

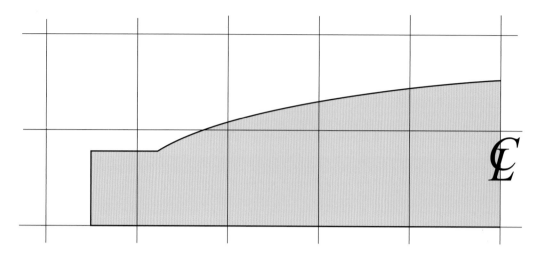

Figure 4-1: Curved upper crosspiece. It is a little long to allow for inevitable slippage during bending. Trim the completed part to fit when you put the back together.

This form should be about 3″ (76mm) thick. Can be made by putting two 2x4's together.
Only the lower form is needed for hot bending. Use both for glue-up bending.

Enlarge with 2″ (51mm) squares

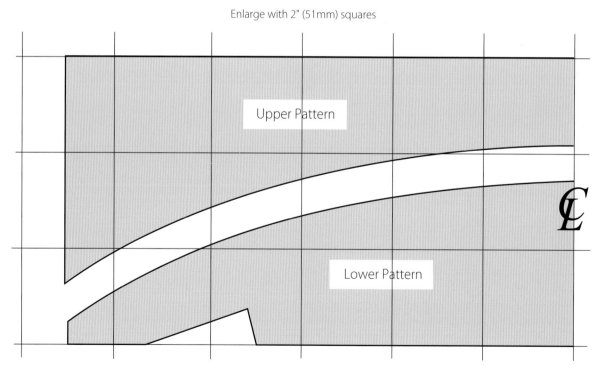

Figure 4-2: Upper crosspiece bending forms. Hot bending uses only the lower form, but glue-lam bending requires both. Make them the same thickness, as the curved back is wide.

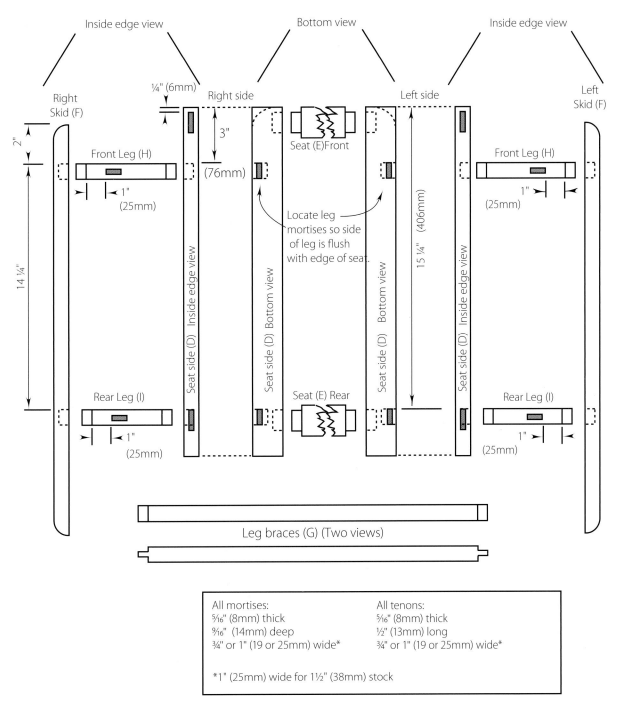

Figure 4-3: **Seat mortises and tenons.** Note that the seat sides are shown in two views. Dimensions given are for mortise or tenon locations. For exact length of the parts, consult the parts list.

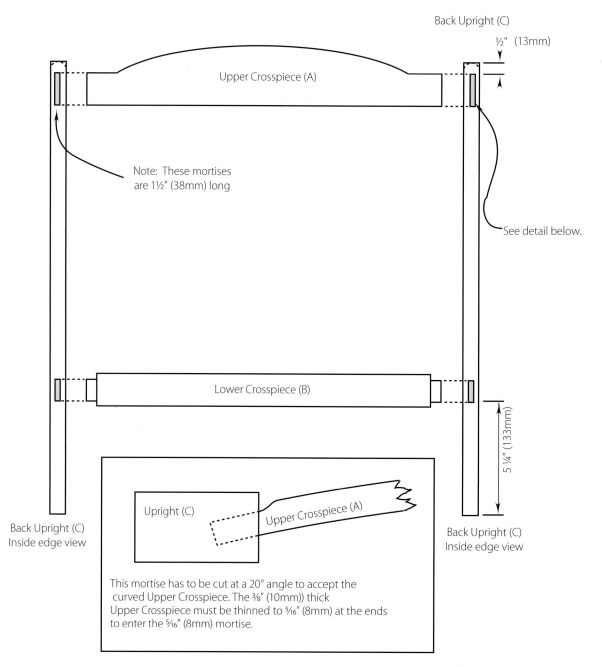

Back Upright (C)

½" (13mm)

Upper Crosspiece (A)

Note: These mortises are 1½" (38mm) long

See detail below.

Lower Crosspiece (B)

5 ¼" (133mm)

Back Upright (C)
Inside edge view

Upright (C)

Upper Crosspiece (A)

This mortise has to be cut at a 20° angle to accept the curved Upper Crosspiece. The ⅜" (10mm)) thick Upper Crosspiece must be thinned to ⁵⁄₁₆" (8mm) at the ends to enter the ⁵⁄₁₆" (8mm) mortise.

Back Upright (C)
Inside edge view

Figure 4-4: Back mortises and tenons. Detail is of the curved back as it enters the back upright.

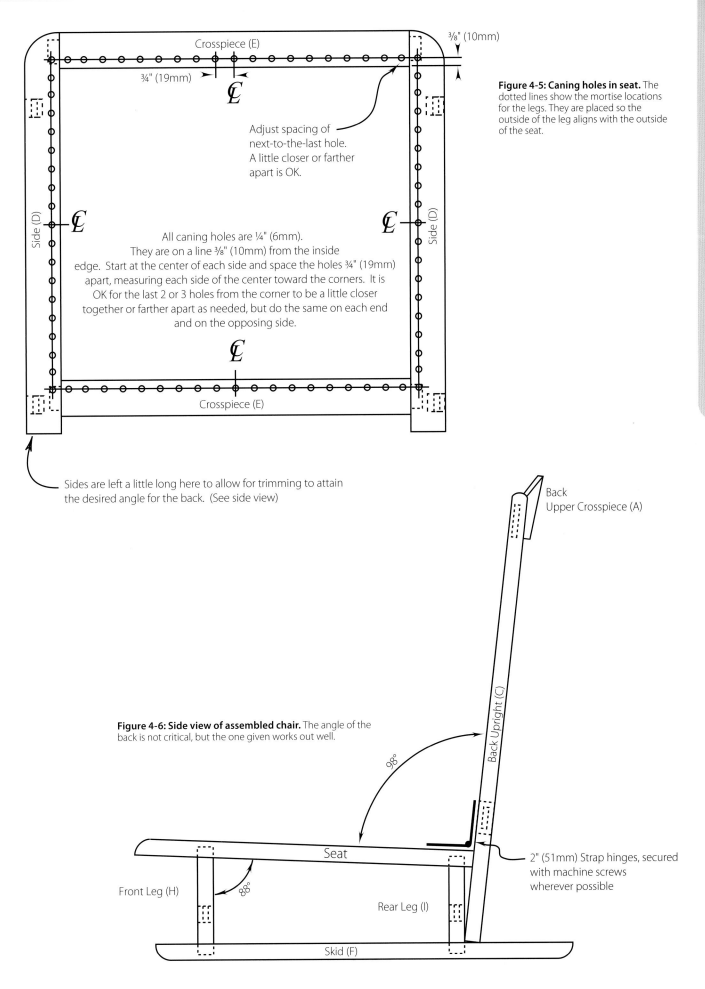

Crosspiece (E)

¾" (19mm)

⅜" (10mm)

Adjust spacing of next-to-the-last hole. A little closer or farther apart is OK.

Side (D)

Side (D)

All caning holes are ¼" (6mm). They are on a line ⅜" (10mm) from the inside edge. Start at the center of each side and space the holes ¾" (19mm) apart, measuring each side of the center toward the corners. It is OK for the last 2 or 3 holes from the corner to be a little closer together or farther apart as needed, but do the same on each end and on the opposing side.

Crosspiece (E)

Figure 4-5: Caning holes in seat. The dotted lines show the mortise locations for the legs. They are placed so the outside of the leg aligns with the outside of the seat.

Sides are left a little long here to allow for trimming to attain the desired angle for the back. (See side view)

Back Upper Crosspiece (A)

Back Upright (C)

98°

Figure 4-6: Side view of assembled chair. The angle of the back is not critical, but the one given works out well.

Seat

Front Leg (H)

88°

Rear Leg (I)

2" (51mm) Strap hinges, secured with machine screws wherever possible

Skid (F)

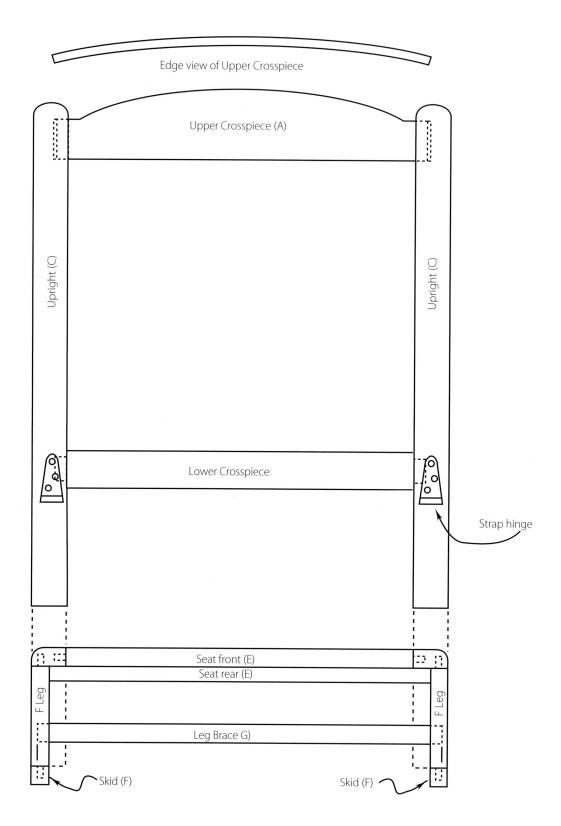

Figure 4-7: Front view of the chair.

Protecting Your Hands

Camp cooks always end up handling a variety of hot objects. Your pan holders from home just won't stand up to the heavy-duty use of camp cooking; being too close to the fire will singe and burn them, or they will get a bit wet and lose their effectiveness.

The best solution I have found is the heavy leather gloves that welders use. They can be found at welding supply stores. They are also available, sometimes in more colorful versions, from stove shops. These gloves with their long gauntlets will allow you to reach right down in front of the fire to tend a reflector oven, or to handle a hot pot of boiling water. Designed for handling hot steel, these gloves give great protection from burns and will last the average outdoorsman a lifetime.

Welder's gloves are useful for handling hot stuff around the campfire and reaching down between the oven and the fire when necessary. Those are Maine Guide Breakfast Buns in the oven.

Maine Guide Breakfast Buns

These buns go great with any breakfast where a bread is called for. The recipe given makes 24 buns, but it is easy to reduce or increase the batch size. I often use leftover buns for lunch to stretch the Canoe Country Bread.

4 cups biscuit mix
2 or 3 tablespoons of cooking oil
2 eggs
Sugar-cinnamon mix
½ box of raisins

Stir the dry ingredients, the wet ingredients, raisins, and enough water to make a thick dough. When it is well mixed, drop by the spoonful on a baking sheet and then sprinkle with sugar-cinnamon mix. Bake in a reflector until golden brown.

You can omit any ingredient but the biscuit mix without seriously affecting the outcome. Not having any spare eggs is no excuse: make it without them. Or try substituting ingredients you do have; use up whatever is on hand, including fresh fruit.

Chapter 5

PACK FRAME

For many years, my pack of choice for personal gear was a pack frame with a compartmented bag. I liked the convenience of separate compartments, which made it easy to organize and locate items. Even after the great dry bags came along, I resisted them for a long time because I disliked the idea of throwing everything into one big open space. Eventually I finally gave in and bought a large dry bag, and worked out a packing system. But my pack frame still remains a useful and valued tool.

I bought and used aluminum pack frames, but they didn't spend much time doing what they were designed for—riding on the back of a human. Instead, mine mostly leaned against the thwart of a canoe or a tree when ashore. They received rough treatment, being pulled, pushed, and twisted into tight places as we packed, unpacked, portaged, etc. After a couple of years of this treatment, the aluminum welds started to break and I needed to replace the frame.

Having learned something about wood bending from my snowshoe-building experience (recounted in my book *Building Wooden Snowshoes & Snowshoe Furniture*, also published by Fox Chapel Publishing), I decided to try making a wood pack frame. I reasoned that it should last at least as long as the aluminum ones, and in the meantime, I would have the satisfaction of using yet another piece of self-made gear. Several years passed before I realized that I had not had to replace a frame in a long time. I looked the wood frame over closely and decided I had stumbled on a winner the first time out: the frame showed no signs of failure. Only surface wear from rough handling gave evidence of the years of use.

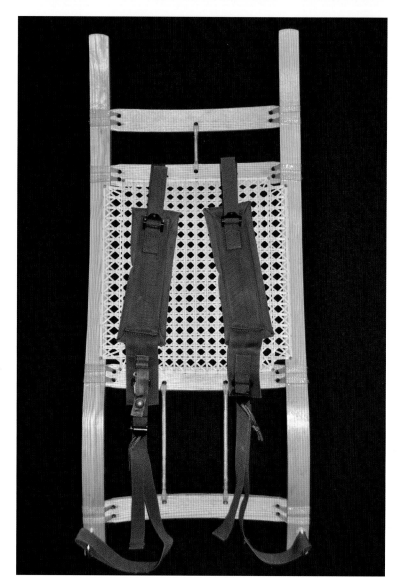

Sturdy and useful, pack frames like this one have served me well.

The durability of this pack frame comes from the flexibility of the wood and the nylon-fastened mortise and tenon joints. There are no glued joints, so the frame can bend and twist with stress, yet it returns to its original shape because of the tightly wrapped nylon fastenings. People of the far north who needed strong, lightweight, flexible sleds for dogs to pull have used this fastening method for centuries. Modern mushers still use the same time-honored principle for their sleds. The only change I made was replacing the rawhide they had to use with more durable and easily obtainable nylon line.

Serious backpackers—the ones who cut off their toothbrush handles to save weight—will not be interested in this pack frame. But if you are an outdoor person who needs a sturdy and dependable pack frame for all-round use, you will be hard pressed to find anything better than this hardwood frame.

Materials

- Hot-bending method
- 2 pieces ¾" x 1 ½" x 37" (19 x 38 x 940mm) (uprights)
- 4 pieces ⅜" x 1 ½" x 20" (10 x 38 x 508mm) (crossbars)
- Glue-bending method
- 8 pieces ³⁄₁₆" x 1 ⅝" x 37" (5 x 41 x 940mm) (uprights)
- 12 pieces ⅛" x 1 ⅝" x 20" (3 x 38 x 508mm) (crossbars)
- 2 standard 2x4x8s (38 x 89 x 2,440mm) for bending forms (one is enough for hot bending)
- Water-resistant glue
- Nylon mason's line
- 500 or more feet of medium plastic cane
- 10 or more feet of plastic binder cane
- 1 quart exterior polyurethane

Tools

- Hot water container (for hot bending—not needed for glue bending)
- Several clamps (see photos)
- Table saw
- Chisel or router for making mortises
- Rule or tape measure
- Drill and drill bits
- Square
- Sandpaper

Jason demonstrates how easy it is to pack an outboard motor, which would otherwise be an uncomfortable task. The frame would be equally handy for packing out a moose quarter (okay, a small moose quarter) or any other bulky, heavy item.

Making a Frame

Just about any clear hardwood with a reasonably straight grain will work for the pack frame. I have most often used ash, because that was the type of wood I had the most of, but I have also used maple, birch, and cherry with good results.

You may need to adjust the frame dimensions to fit yourself. I am about 6'1" (1,855mm), and I made my frame big enough to be used as a "freighter frame," as some describe them. To make the frame shorter or longer, I recommend modifying the bending pattern in the middle of the frame—that is, the area that will be caned or have the rope braces. The curve is gentle there, so it is simple to shorten or extend the pattern. Change the dimensions in **Figure 5-1** by whatever you decide, thus changing the entire frame by the same amount.

1. Cut and bend the pieces.

You have a choice of two bending methods— hot-bending or glue-bending. I have used both with equally good results.

Option 1: Hot-bend. You will need a container at least 37" (940mm) long to accommodate the uprights for the wood boiling. Start by making only the bottom part of the bending forms from **Figures**

5-2 and **5-3**. If you make the bending forms wide enough, you should be able to bend the two upright pieces at once, eliminating the long drying time while waiting to reuse the forms. (The bending form for the crossbars is the same as for the canoe chair back. That is why it is so long; the finished crossbars will be less than 14" [345mm].) If you make two of the crossbar bending forms, using two 2 by 4s (38 x 89mm) for each, you should be able to bend all four of the crossbars in one bending session (two on each form).

Cut the frame parts, boil the water, and insert the parts. After about two hours, carefully remove the wood, place it on the bending form, and quickly clamp it in place. I recommend padding your clamps, so they don't dent the hot wood while it is soft. Allow the wood to dry for several days before removing the clamps. Clean up the pieces as needed.

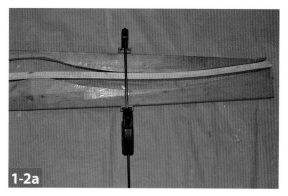

Glue and stack the upright strips.
Put the stack in the upright form before the glue dries. Get the two parts of the form close enough that the heavy-duty clamps can complete the bending.

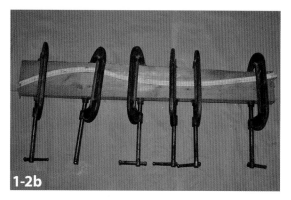

Clamp and let dry.
An upright needs to stay in the bending form only a couple of hours before you can remove it and use the form again for the second upright.

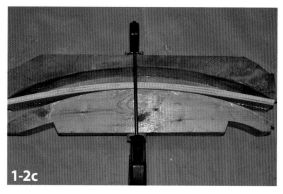

Glue and stack the crosspiece strips.
Here we are doing two at once. Look closely and you'll see glue squeezing out from between the two pieces.

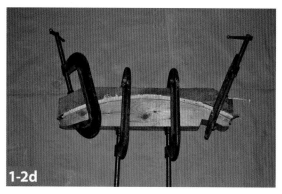

Clamp and let dry.

Option 2: Glue-bend.

Make both the top and bottom of the bending forms on **Figures 5-2** and **5-3**. Then rip the wood frame material to the dimensions specified in the materials list. The ³⁄₁₆" (5mm)-thick strips are ⅛" (3mm) wider than the finished part will be because there is bound to be some slippage as you squeeze the pieces together, and the excess will allow you to trim the finished part to its final size of 1½" (38mm) wide. Coat all of the facing pieces of the strips with a thin coat of glue and stack them. I like to use Water Resistant Titebond II Glue; it is available almost everywhere and does a great job. Because this project won't be submerged in water for an extended period (we hope!), it isn't necessary to use waterproof epoxy glue.

When the stack is ready, before the glue dries, place it between the top and bottom bending forms and squeeze them together as evenly as possible with clamps. As you pull them together, watch for slippage and correct as needed. Sometimes temporarily putting a clamp over the edges helps keep the pieces from sliding out of line with each other. This method doesn't require a long drying time; within a 24-hour period you can have all pieces bent and ready to finish. For example, I bent one upright and two crossbars in the morning, placing them side-by-side on the bending form. They stuck together, but it was simple to cut them apart later on the table saw. I removed them and bent the remaining pieces after the evening news, and the following day was ready to cut them to the final dimensions, clean them up, and start the assembly process.

Determining the Mortise Angle for Curved Pieces

The angle at which a curved piece fits into its mortise can vary slightly because of differences in making up the pattern for the bending. Also, the angle changes with the length of the curved piece, so if you opt to make something a little larger or smaller than is described, you will need to find a new angle. At any rate, it is good to know how to determine the angle needed. Refer to the photos and follow these steps:

1. Cut the curved piece to (or very close to) the finished length.

2. Lay a square on a piece of paper and draw a vertical line (A) and a horizontal line (B).

3. Place the curved piece on the paper with both ends resting against the horizontal leg of the square.

4. Draw a short line (about 1" [25mm]) along the end of the curved piece where it will eventually enter the mortise.

5. Remove the square and the curved piece and draw line C by extending the short line drawn in step 4 so it crosses line B and is long enough to be measured.

6. Draw a line (D) that is parallel to Line A and intersects the intersection of lines B and C.

7. Measure the angle between Line B and Line C. In this case the angle is 12°, which is the angle we used for the pack frame mortises.

Draw lines A and B.

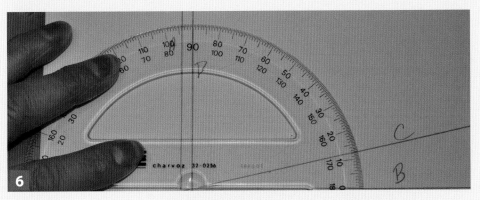

Draw line D.

Assembling a Frame

2. Make angled mortises in the uprights.

Figure 5-1 shows the mortise positions. The mortises in the uprights need to be at a 12° angle, but you should check it on your own crosspieces in case there are variations. See the sidebar on page 55. Photo 5 on page 41 shows one method of cutting the mortises at the correct angle. I recommend clamping mortises at the proper angle before starting if you intend to cut them by hand. That way, you can work vertically without thinking about the angle. Cut the ⁵⁄₁₆" (8mm) mortises ½" (13mm) deep and 1 ½" (38mm) long. Be careful to get the mortises angled in the right direction. I like to make a mark on the end indicating the proper angle. With the piece at an angle in the vise, the mark is vertical—then I know the angle is correct. More than one nicely bent piece of wood has been ruined by carelessness in cutting angled mortises. A hint: If the angle setup is the same for both uprights, then the uprights will face opposite directions as their mortises are cut. That is, if the bottom of the first upright is to your left as you cut your mortises, then the bottom of the second upright should be to your right.

3. Determine the length of the crosspieces, and cut them.

Lay the uprights side-by-side 15" (381mm) apart measured to the outside (see **Figure 5-1**); if your frame is to be wider, adjust them accordingly. Measure for the length of the crosspieces, then

cut them. They should be cut to 13" (330mm) if everything you have done is according to the plan, but check. It is better to cut them a little long and then trim them than to cut them too short. Measure the length of the crosspieces in a straight line, not over the curve. Also, find the center of the crosspieces and measure 6½" (165mm) or whatever each way from that point so you end up with a nice even curve.

4. Thin the ends of the crosspieces and insert them in the mortises.

Thin the ends of the crosspieces, which will go into the mortises, to ⁵⁄₁₆" (8mm). I do this with a drum sander, but use whatever tool you have on hand that will handle the job. Once they are at the proper thickness, do the final fitting with a sharp knife. When all of the crosspieces are fitted in place, squeeze the uprights together with clamps and check the distance from outside to outside of the uprights. It should be 15" (381mm) unless you are making your pack frame a different size. Adjust as needed. Clean up all the wood parts if you have not already.

5. Drill holes for the nylon line and sand as needed.

When you are satisfied with the fit of the crosspieces, it is time to tie everything together. Drill two ¼" (6mm) holes 1" (25mm) from the ends and ½" (13mm) apart on each end of each crosspiece. While you are at it, mark and drill ¼" (6mm) holes for the rope braces as shown in **Figure 5-1**. If you are going to cane the center section, you can omit the holes for the two angle braces. After drilling, do any final sanding that is needed. Get rid of all the pencil and tool marks; they are difficult to remove later.

6. Clamp the parts in place and tie them together.

Clamp all the parts in place and use a square to make sure the crosspieces are at 90° to the uprights. Adjust as needed. Do not glue the joints. Wind nylon mason's line tightly through the holes and around the uprights. This makes the joints solid and secure, but

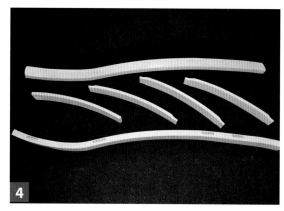

4

Thin the ends of the crosspieces. The ends of three of these crosspieces have already been thinned to ⁵⁄₁₆" (8mm), and the mortises cut in one of the uprights. All of the wood pieces are bent and cleaned up, so once that fourth crosspiece's ends are trimmed and the other mortises cut, this frame will be ready for assembly.

still allows the frame a degree of flexibility. Start the wrap by tucking the end under the first wrap. Finish by tucking the end under the last loop, and cut the line to about ¼" (6mm). Then melt it with a flame and flatten the melted glob against the wrap. This makes a smooth, lump-free fastening. I found 12 to 14 wraps around the upright, using both holes, to be about right, but this can vary with different size line. The main thing is to pull each wrap as tight as you can.

When all of the crosspieces are bound in place, remove the clamps and construct rope braces by using the same nylon mason's line to make six passes through the holes, which will create a bundle of 12 lines. Then, with the same line, wrap the bundle from one end to the other, finishing by tucking the end under the last loop and melting as described above. If you intend to cane the center section you do not need the two angled rope braces shown in **Figure 5-1**.

Cane the seat. Because the corner holes cannot be drilled, Kelly modified the usual technique for finishing the corners. Sometimes you can use one of the lacing holes for cane as well, which works the cane a little closer to the upright. Neither option alters the comfort value of the caned pack frame.

7. Drill the caning holes.

(If you do not intend to cane the center section, skip to Step 8.) The line of ¼" (6mm) holes will be ⅜" (10mm) from the inside edge and ¾" (19mm) apart. On each of the four sides, find the center and then space the holes in each direction from that point, ensuring that each hole has a mate on the opposite side. Note that because of the nylon binding there will not be corner holes.

Finishing a Frame

8. Sand and finish the frame.

Give the frame a final sanding, and then apply two or three coats of quality exterior polyurethane. Pay special attention to the nylon binding and ropes, using plenty of polyurethane so it thoroughly soaks the nylon. If your frame does not lay flat after you have finished the bindings, coat only the bindings with polyurethane and clamp it down flat while it dries. That usually takes out the twist, and then you can go ahead and polyurethane the rest of the frame until you are satisfied with the finish.

9. Follow the caning instructions beginning on page 24.

(If you do not intend to cane the center section, skip to Step 10.) As noted, the only exception to the step-by-step caning instructions is that the pack frame doesn't have corner holes or angled sides. The lack of corner holes isn't a big deal because they are mostly cosmetic anyway. See how Kelly handled this in one of the corners.

10. Attach the straps and pack.

How you attach the straps and pack will depend on the design of the ones you buy. The ones I used are shown in the photo on page 58; the source is listed in "Resources and Supplies." I passed the upper straps through a slot cut in the crosspiece and attached the lower strap using a small U-bolt. I have had no luck finding ready-made pack bags to go on the pack frame. The bag shown in photo 10 was

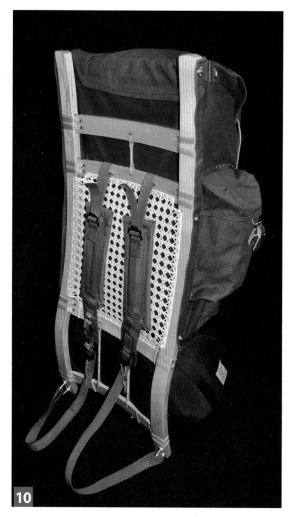

10

Attach the straps and pack. Because I had no luck locating a ready-made bag to go on the frame, I commissioned Jane Barron of Alder Stream Canvas to make one (see "Resources and Supplies"). Attach a bag like this one as shown, using wood screws directly into the outside of the uprights.

made by Jane Barron of Alder Stream Canvas. Her contact information is in "Resources and Supplies." The lack of a bag does not diminish the frame's usefulness, however. (See photo on page 53.) Some people like to stretch a piece of canvas across the lower section where it rests on the small of the back. This holds the frame itself away from the body. Others opt for a padded belt, which does the same thing, as well placing some of the load weight on the hips.

I wish I could tell you how long your frame should last, but I can't because I have never worn out one. I do foresee that one might want to touch up the polyurethane a little before passing the frame along to the grandchildren. To that end, one last bit of advice: write your name and the date somewhere on the frame. Your handiwork could mean a lot to a descendant someday.

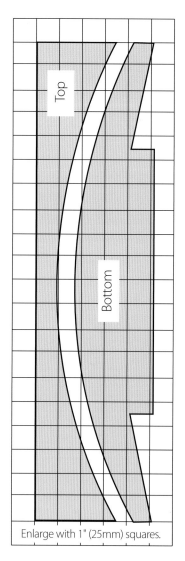

Enlarge with 1" (25mm) squares.

Figure 5-3: Crosspiece bending forms.
If you made or will make the canoe chair, you can use the same form that bends the chair back to bend the packframe crosspieces. Because the pack frame crosspieces are shorter than the chair back, the angle of entry into the mortises will be different. Refer to the sidebar on page 55.

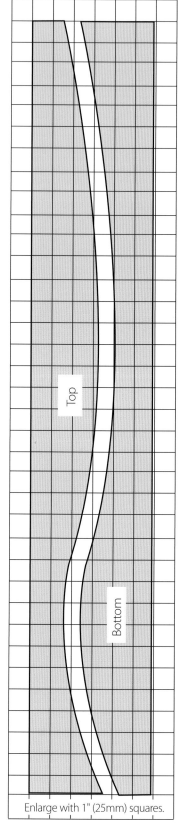

Enlarge with 1" (25mm) squares.

Figure 5-2: Upright bending forms.
The glue-lam method uses both parts, but the hot bend method requires only the bottom one.

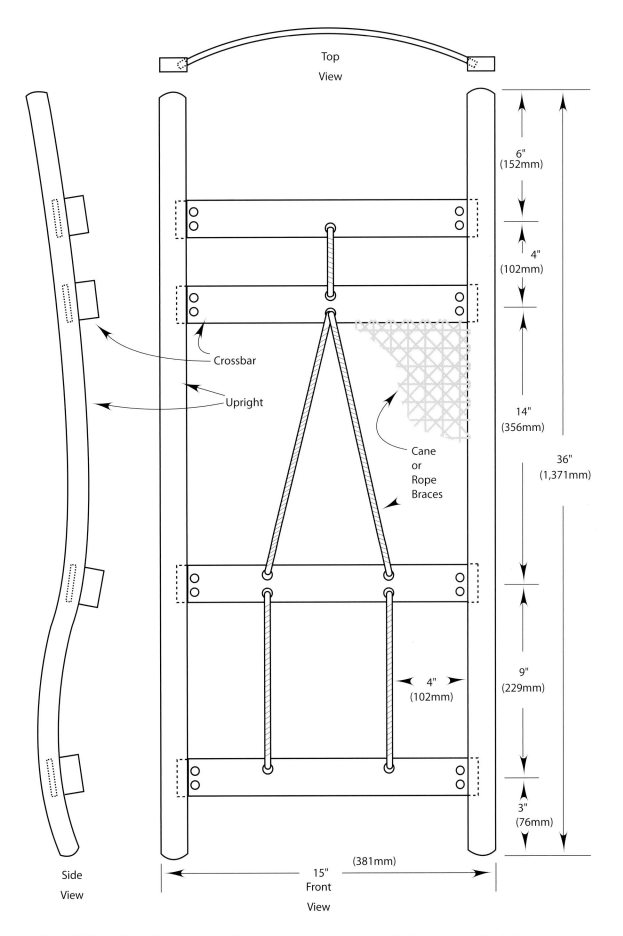

Top
View

6"
(152mm)

4"
(102mm)

Crossbar

Upright

Cane
or
Rope
Braces

14"
(356mm)

36"
(1,371mm)

9"
(229mm)

4"
(102mm)

3"
(76mm)

Side
View

(381mm)

15"
Front
View

Figure 5-1: Three views of the frame. Includes locations of the crosspieces and reinforcing rope braces. You don't need the two angled rope braces if you cane the center area.

These paddles are beautiful—but more importantly, they are supremely functional. Woodburning optional.

Chapter 6

PADDLES

Ever since I first started building cedar strip canoes in the early 1970s, I wanted to take the next step and build paddles to go along with them. The logical thing was to make them of cedar strips—that being the construction method of the canoe and, besides, there is usually some cedar left over when the canoe is finished.

It wasn't until I discovered and started to use epoxy technology that I was able to make a paddle that would stand up to the rigors of year-in and year-out canoeing on Maine's wilderness rivers. This paddle design has proven itself to be unbelievably tough, lightweight, and durable. My guests and I have given it many years of hard use. I was surprised to discover recently that I was still using one of

the first paddles I ever made using the methods described in this chapter—surprised because most of my guests were new to canoeing. They were likely to use the paddle like a pole to get off a gravel bar or like a pry-bar to extricate themselves when they get stuck on a rock in whitewater. Not to say they are indestructible—we break one now and then. Like most other things, there is wear and tear that has to be repaired occasionally, but I have not found a manufactured paddle to compare to them for strength, lightness, and flexibility. To all this, add the pride of making your own custom paddle, and you have a project that is hard to beat for the serious outdoor person.

Familiarize yourself with the parts of a paddle (see **Figures 6-1** and **6-2**). Start by making a full-size copy of the patterns (blade, grip, and spine, **Figures 6-4** and **6-5**). Make the grip area large enough to accommodate whatever grip you wish to make. The grip and shaft is cut to final size when the lamination is complete. The length of the shaft is up to you. Most canoeists agree that a paddle should be long enough to reach somewhere between the standing paddler's chin and nose. I am 6' 1" (1,850mm) tall and prefer a paddle 63" (1,600mm) long (chin high).

Forms

You will need a piece of plywood—½" (13mm) or thicker—to lay out and tack down your cedar strips. Make an outline of your paddle on this plywood. Cover it with plastic so that the strips will not be glued to it. You will cover the outline with the strips as you glue them up. This is an easy way to ensure the glued-up blade (with the oversize shaft and grip) is large enough to cut out your blade when the glue is dry. Completed blades and the plywood base are shown on page 63.

The jig for gluing up the spines (the core that becomes the handle and the center of the paddle) is shown in **Figure 6-3**. As shown, it will glue up a pair of spines (enough for one paddle) at once. All that is needed besides the jig are the clamps to pull it together. Be sure to use plastic between the spines and between the spines and the jig. The three bolts slide along the slots in the base and keep the slider and the spines from buckling when pressure is applied with the clamps. That's all you will need in the way of forms; the rest of the materials will be part of the paddle itself.

Blade thickness

The paddle blade is to be ¼" (6mm) thick when it is ready to be laminated to the spines. If you have a surface planer available, it is easier to start out with strips that are ⅜" (10mm) thick. Plane the whole thing to ¼" (6mm) after the gluing is done. If your smoothing has to be done by hand or with a sander, then start with strips that are ¼" (6mm), maybe a little more, and then work them down to ¼" (6mm) when dry. The width of the strips is not important. Usually, they are ¾" or ⅞" (19 or 22mm) because that is the thickness of the boards they are sawn from. Since this is a flat project, wider strips would be perfectly OK.

Materials

- 1 piece plywood, ½" (13mm) or more thick, 12" x 72" (300 x 1,800mm)
- 4 pieces ¾" x 2" x 60" (19 x 51 x 1,500mm) (hardwood preferred)
- Polyethylene plastic (enough to liberally cover the plywood)
- 12 wood screws, #8 x 1¼" (32mm)
- 1 package of ⁹⁄₁₆" (14mm) staples
- 2 or more straight pins (like for sewing)
- 10 (about) cedar strips ⅜" x ¾" (10mm x 19mm), length depends on paddle length. Some will be cut shorter.
- 1 hardwood strip ⅜" x ¾" (10mm x 19mm), same length as cedar strips
- 6 cedar strips ½" x ¾" (13mm x 19mm), length depends on paddle length. Make 12" (305mm) shorter than paddle.
- 2 hardwood strips ¼" x ½" (6mm x 13mm), same length as above.
- Small container of carpenter's glue
- Epoxy and hardener
- Cotton fibers for glue
- Silica
- 6 disposable glue brushes
- Sandpaper, 60, 80 and 120 grits
- 5 feet (1.5m) of ¼" or ⅛" (6mm or 3mm) braided nylon cord
- 3 or 4 throwaway brushes, 2" (51mm)
- 2 pieces 6 ounce (or lighter) fiberglass cloth, approximately 12" x 26" (305mm x 660mm)
- Steel wool, #00
- 1-quart polyurethane varnish with ultra violet filter

Tools

- Screwdriver
- Surface planer (optional)
- Table saw**
- Stapler (tacker) capable of holding ⁹⁄₁₆" (14mm) staples
- 6 or 8 "C" clamps (more would be better)
- Hammer
- Electric sander (optional)
- Band saw, jig saw, or similar method to cut curved lines
- Rasp, 4-in-1
- Hand plane
- Disk sander*
- Carpenter's rule
- Pencil
- Router with ⅜" (10mm) radius rounding bit (optional)
- 1 or 2 plastic squeegees

** Necessary, but limited use—borrow or beg if you don't have one.

Spines

The thickness of the spines should be ⅜" or ⁷⁄₁₆" (10 or 11mm) (your choice) when they are ready to laminate to the blade, so the same thing applies here as to the blade. If you have access to a surface planer, make them ½" or ⁹⁄₁₆" (13 or 14mm) and plane them to thickness when ready. Otherwise, make them close enough to the finished size that you will not have to remove an excessive amount of wood by hand to prepare them for further lamination. If you think you may need a paddle with a stronger than usual shaft, then you can make the spines a little thicker. You then make the shaft oblong in shape instead of perfectly round (see **Figure 6-2**). This gives the extra thickness where the pressure is likely to be applied, but adds very little weight.

I should mention here that early on in the development of these paddles we made the spines of solid ash, ⅜" (10mm) thick. This produced a paddle that was strong, somewhat flexible, but a little heavy. If weight is not a factor for you then you can go this route and somewhat simplify the lamination process.

Wood selection

Most of the strips for your paddle will be made from cedar—that makes the paddle light. But there are a few very important strips made of ash, or other strong hardwood—they make your paddle strong. These hardwood strips are arranged to form an *X* in the finished paddle shaft. Look at the cross-section of the paddle shaft in **Figure 6-2**. The hardwoods I have had good success with are ash, cherry, maple, and birch. The cherry gives a nice contrasting color that fits in well with some paddles. Just keep in mind the goals of lightness, strength, and flexibility.

There is one hardwood strip right in the middle of the paddle blade. Make it the same size as the cedar strips that make up the rest of the blade. The hardwood strip in the spines needs to be the same thickness as the strips, but only ¼" (6mm) wide. This might be a little confusing, because in this reference the thickness is greater than the width. At any rate, you will be using hardwood strips that are ⁹⁄₁₆" (14mm) (or whatever the thickness of your spines are to be) x ¼" (6mm). The ¼" (6mm) hardwood strip for the spines can be seen in **Figure 6-2** and in photos 3a and 3b.

Gathering Wood for Campfires

I have read books on camping that start the section on campfires with something like "Gather a supply of dry hardwood…." If you live where evergreens predominate, as I do, lots of luck finding dry hardwood! There is little hardwood in the first place, so the chance of finding some dead and dry is small. Pioneers crossing the Great Plains used buffalo chips—a far cry from "dry, hard wood." The point is that you use what's available and make do. Foresters label my part of the country as spruce/fir forest. So, spruce and fir are what we have for camping firewood. Sometimes some white cedar is available if it happens to be growing near the camp site.

The only way to know what dry wood is best in your area is to try them. With a little practice you can control the heat of your fire nearly as effectively as if you had a little knob to turn as you do on the kitchen range back home. For example, I have found that dry fir and cedar give a bright, hot blaze just right for reflector baking, but it doesn't last long. Spruce yields a more subdued fire that comes closer to burning like hardwood, with coals that can last for a while and make a better fire for cooking.

Laminating

1. Attach the strips.

The lamination process has to be done in stages. First, you glue up the paddle blade. This is done with ordinary carpenter's glue. These non-waterproof glues can be used here because none of the wood involved will be exposed to water. Lay the ash or other hardwood strip down to establish your paddle centerline and then glue on enough cedar strips to cover your paddle outline. You can staple as you go or place staples only on the outside strips of the blade. It doesn't matter where you staple on the shaft and grip area because these areas are all going to be covered by the spines.

The photo at right shows the stapling being done so as to eliminate staple holes in the finished blade. This is strictly a cosmetic choice and nothing more. The absence of staple holes does make a nice clean surface if you plan any decoration of the blade. Sometimes it is necessary to pull the strips together with a clamp before stapling the outside strip of the paddle blade. The clamp can be left in place until the glue has set up.

2. Complete the drying process.

The glue used for the blade will set up in an hour or so, and at that time it is a good idea to pull it from your form and stand it up to complete the drying process. The reason for doing this is that the glue trapped between the paddle blade and the plastic will not dry very fast. The moisture in the glue will cause the thin strips to warp, causing an extreme cup in the blade. By removing the paddle as soon as possible, and letting the whole thing dry evenly, it will remain flat. Do not pull the staples now, because the glue may not be completely set up.

Attach the strips. Staple the ⅜" (10mm) strips to the mounting board, which has an outline of the paddle with a centerline so you know where to start. The center hardwood strip here is cherry.

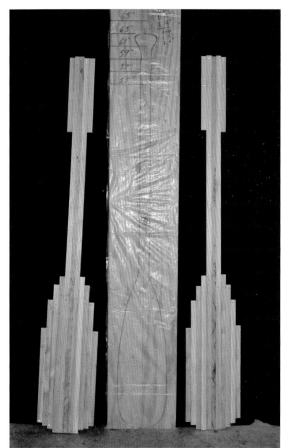

Complete the drying process. Avoid leaving the paddles on the board too long. Remove the paddle(s) after about an hour and allow them to finish drying. Here we did a paddle on each side of the mounting board.

3a

Glue up the spines. The spines for one paddle are shown in the clamping jig. Each spine consists of two pieces of cedar ½" (13mm)-thick x ¾" (19mm)-wide and one piece of hardwood ¼" (6mm) x ½" (13mm). To use the clamping jig, it is important that all pieces be uniform in size. There is plastic between the spine and the jig and between the two spines.

3. Apply the spines.

The spines are glued up with epoxy glue made with epoxy resin thickened with cotton fibers. This waterproof glue is needed because the spine will be exposed to the elements. Mix your glue no thicker than necessary to do the job and spread a liberal layer on each strip where they meet. A disposable brush can be used to spread the glue.

Cover both surfaces of the spine parts with epoxy glue before putting them into the clamping jig—this means coating one surface of the cedar strips and both sides of the hardwood center strip. Place the glued-up spine on plastic into the jig and then place another piece of plastic on top of the first spine and repeat the process to make your second spine. When both spines are in place, use several clamps to pull the slider into the spines. Excessive pressure is not necessary and is not recommended. As you tighten the slider, tap the spines with a hammer to ensure they are in alignment. When you do this, simply fold a piece of plastic over the top spine so the glue does not splash or foul up your hammer. Allow the glue of all three components (blade and two spines) to cure overnight or at least 24 hours.

4. Remove the staples and smooth.

Pull the staples from the blade and shaft. Now take all three components and bring them down to the desired thickness with a surface planer, by hand, a sander, or what-have-you. The surfaces need to be as flat as possible to make for good lamination contact as you continue the process.

3b

Clamp the spines. Here is the spine-clamping jig with spines for two paddles.

5

Saw out the blade. Trace the paddle blade by aligning the centerline of the pattern with the center of the hardwood strip. Only cut out the blade at this time. Leave the shaft and grip area as-is for now.

5. Saw out the blade.

Next, trace your blade pattern and saw it out on a band saw, jigsaw, or whatever means you have to do this. Leave the shaft and grip area as-is for now.

Shaping the Paddle

1. Sand the paddle.

Remove the clamps, and you now have a very unlikely looking mess that's supposed to become a paddle—but don't worry. Use a sander to clean up the top and bottom so you can mark and cut those areas accurately. Don't worry about the edges where the glue squeezed out; you will cut them away later. Mark the center of the paddle shaft a few inches down from the grip area. This center should be the middle of the ¼" (6mm) hardwood strip. Do the same on the shaft at the throat. Now measure out ½" or ⁹⁄₁₆" (13 or 14mm) from these marks in both directions so you have 1" or 1⅛" (25 or 29mm) between the outside marks. Connect these marks with a straightedge on each side of the shaft so you define a 1" or 1⅛" (25 or 29mm) shaft.

2. Trace in a grip.

With the shaft marked out, select the grip pattern and trace it in the grip area. Adjust the grip pattern so it lines up with the shaft you defined with the straight edge. At the throat, you will need to do a little freehand work on each side to make a smooth, graceful transition from the straight shaft to the rounded blade. When you are satisfied with this and the rest of your marks, go ahead and cut the shaft and grip out with a band saw or whatever means you have to do so.

3. Round over the throat and grip.

Now you have a square paddle shaft that should measure 1" x 1" (25 x 25mm) or 1⅛" x 1⅛" (29 x 29mm), and your grip area has its outline shape. At this point, everything from the throat up to and including the grip should be rounded over. If you have a router with a rounding cutter (⅜" [10mm] radius or thereabouts), this will do the job. However, most of the wood you have to remove is cedar, which is soft and almost fun to take off with a rasp.

4. Shape the shaft.

The paddle shaft, of course, should be round or oblong, but you can take artistic license with the area or you can copy one of the grips shown in chapter. In either case this shaping is more artist than scientific. You can have fun with it by just t off a little wood and trying it until it feels just ri Once you have the shaft and grip down to the you want, you will leave them in the rough and on to complete the paddle blade. This is done this point because the resin used in the process finishing the paddle blade, including the fibergl usually ends up running down the shaft and m up the finish work you might have done, requir that the sanding be done all over again to rem Better to do all your sanding at once.

Trace in a grip. When the epoxy glue has cured, mark ɑ trace out the grip. Where the spine meets the blade, yo to connect the curve of the blade to the straight line yo

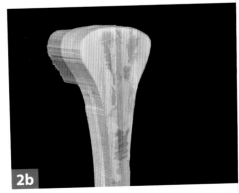

Shape the grip. The grip area is ready for shaping. The over. You can use a router with a rounding cutter, but la wood rasp.

6. Shape the ends of the spines.

You are almost ready to laminate the three components together, but first you should work down the pointed ends of the spines so they look like the one in the photo at right. This shaping could be done when the lamination is complete, but it is a lot easier to do beforehand. You will round and thin out only the top side of each spine, leaving the bottom flat for lamination with the blade. A disk sander or belt sander does a quick job of shaping and thinning. You could also use a hand plane or even a rasp.

7. Make the assembly jig.

With the three components of your paddle sized and shaped, you are ready for the final lamination. The simple holding jig shown in the photo below will make it a lot easier to assemble the paddle parts. It can be made of about any scrap wood you might have around the shop.

8. Laminate the paddle.

Before placing the three components into the holding jig, ensure they are all the same width. This usually means cutting down the paddle shaft to match the width of the spines. Also, cut the paddle and the spines to the desired length. The spines should be 12" (305mm) shorter than the paddle. To get the best bond between the spines and the blade/shaft, be sure to coat both components before bringing them together.

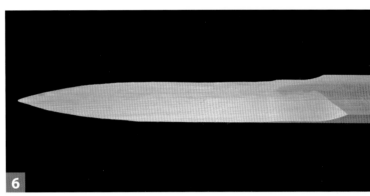

Shape the ends of the spines. The end of the spine extends into the paddle blade. Bring the spines to a point, then taper to a knife-edge, leaving one side flat. Since most of the wood to be removed is soft cedar, a variety of tools will do the job. Here we used a belt sander.

Make the assembly jig. Build a holding jig from scrap wood to hold the paddle as it dries. Before the glue-up, saw the shaft of the paddle to the exact same width as the spines. You can see how this would make things easier to line up. It is important that the center of the spines align with the center of the hardwood strip in the paddle. This creates the X shown in Figure 6-2.

9. Clamp the paddle.

After spreading the glue and placing the parts together, you are ready to clamp them. The first couple of clamps are the hardest, as you hold the parts and try to keep them from slipping out of place. Tighten the clamps carefully as you hold them lined up with each other and you will succeed. It is easiest to put a clamp on each end initially, get the alignment correct, and then place the others in between. You have correct alignment at the top when you look down on the top of the grip and see an *X* formed by the hardwood pieces—like that shown in **Figure 6-2**. The alignment at the blade should have the points of the spines centered on the hardwood strip that runs the length of the paddle blade, shaft, and grip. Do all of your clamping work with the paddle on edge as it is in the holding jig. Finish clamping with enough clamps to bring the parts together without any voids showing anywhere.

The tips (points) of the spines can be clamped firmly against the blade by the clamp system shown in the photo at bottom, right. With this method, you just cover them with plastic or wax paper, put a piece of wood on each side, and then place a clamp on each end of the pieces of wood.

10. Allow the paddle to cure.

When the clamping is finished, allow the paddle to cure right in the holding jig. If you do not leave the paddle to dry on edge, the weight of the clamps will bend the paddle shaft—not the best way to make a bent-shaft paddle. Once the glue has set, the bent shaft will be set as well. If your shaft is not straight in spite of precautions, you can probably correct the situation while the glue is still wet. Simply loosen the clamps slightly, and then give the paddle shaft a little bend to correct the difficulty. You will probably need a helper for this: one person to hold things in place while the other re-tightens the clamps. This correction is seldom necessary.

11. Clean up the glue squeeze-out.

If you plan to shape a grip you will need to glue on the extra wood you will need to shape it out. A scrap piece of cedar is suggested, as it is lightweight and

9a

Clamp the paddle. In the grip area shown here, a make the grip wide enough. The dark wood will a beneath the clamps are just to hold pressure and between them and the paddle).

9b

easily shaped. You will also have to add of wood to each side of the spine in th Make these the same thickness as the s up the squeezed-out glue around the spines where they lay on the paddle b to remove while it is still wet than afte Leave the paddle to cure for 24 hours

Finishing the Blade

1. Sand the blade.

First sand the paddle blade, removing all glue, pencil marks, machine marks, etc. Initial sanding can be done with 60 grit and then finished up with 80 grit. Finer sanding is unnecessary because the fiberglass covers up any sanding scratches that may be left. At the point where the spine lays on the blade, smooth it out with sandpaper so the junction makes a smooth transition from the flat of the blade to the (previously) rounded shape of the pointed tip of the spine. Even though you carefully removed excess glue from this area when it was still wet, there will be some remaining that has to be taken off. As you do this, be careful not to remove wood that should not be removed. The cedar is soft and can be easily sanded too thin. It is normal to have some glue showing at the junction of the two components when finished, but make sure it feels like a smooth transition as you run your fingers over it.

2. Taper the blade edges.

The tip and edges of your paddle blade are going to be protected by nylon rope. Instructions on how to do this will come a little later. You can use ⅛" or ¼" (3 or 6mm) braided nylon for the edging. Both are readily available at hardware stores. This blade edging is mentioned here because if you choose to use ⅛" (3mm) braided nylon cord, it is necessary to make the edges of the blade ⅛" (3mm) thick. This is done by tapering the edges from a point about 1½" to 2" (38 to 51mm) from the edge out to the edge. Take wood off both sides of the blade until the ¼" (6mm) blade tapers gradually down to ⅛" (3mm) at the edges. The taper is quickly done with a power sander and 50-grit sandpaper on the soft cedar. If done smoothly and gradually, this taper will not be apparent to the eye. It is important to have the edge thickness match that of the nylon cord to ensure a good bond between the fiberglass and the nylon cord. Of course, if you use the thicker, ¼" (6mm) nylon, tapering will be unnecessary. I have used both thicknesses with good results. I prefer the ¼" (6mm) braided nylon.

3. Decorate the paddle.

Since prehistoric times, people have been inclined to decorate the tools and other objects that make up their daily lives. In these days of mass production, this practice has diminished except among those who still make their own tools. If you make your own paddle, you are one of those exceptional people. What better way to express yourself, and personalize your paddle, than to do your own design on its broad flat surface? Further, your work will be sealed and protected by the tough and transparent layer of epoxied fiberglass so it will be about as permanent as such things can get. If you wish to do artwork on your paddle, such as woodburning like that shown in the photos on page 74, now is the time to do it. When you finish, proceed with the next step.

4. Prepare to apply the nylon cord.

You will seal the paddle blade and apply the nylon edge in one operation. Find a spot where you can clamp your paddle in an upright position with the grip on the floor (a.k.a., upside down). Cut the nylon rope to length to reach from throat to throat. However, the part of the blade that needs the most protection is the tip, so it is acceptable to cover just that area if you wish. This will require only 12" to 15" (305 to 381mm) of nylon cord. You will also need two or more straight pins (those used for sewing). You'll see why a little later, but for now leave them sticking up in a piece of scrap wood so they will be easy to pick up with slippery, resin-covered, gloved fingers.

5. Mix some resin.

When everything else is ready to go, put on a pair of protective gloves and mix up a few ounces of resin. Try to estimate enough to cover the blade like varnish and a little extra. The amount needed for these various jobs takes a little practice, but it is always possible to mix up a little more if you run out, so it is OK to be conservative.

6a

Saturate the cord with resin. A piece of braided nylon rope makes a super protection for the edge of your paddle blade.

6. Saturate the cord.

When the resin and hardener are thoroughly mixed, drop the nylon cord into it and cover it with resin so it will be thoroughly soaked when you are finished with the sealing. The blade is sealed by simply painting on a fairly generous coating of resin (use a throw-away brush). You want it to soak in and seal up the pores of the wood so that the resin used in fiberglassing, later on, will not soak into the wood and leave the fiberglass dry. Apply the sealer to the entire blade up to the throat. This is as far as the fiberglass will go.

Foam Brushes vs Chip Brushes

Foam brushes work fine for two or three minutes to apply resin to a project. After that, the glue holding the brush together starts to break down and the brush falls apart. Throwaway bristle brushes (sold as "chip brushes") are a better choice for longer operations.

6b

Use pins to secure the rope. Using common dressmaker's pins, secure the ends of the rope to the blade near the throat area. Allow it all to cure at least 24 hours, and then remove the pins and taper the ends of the rope so they blend into the throat.

7. Apply the nylon cord to the blade edge.

When the blade is completely covered with resin, including the edges, clamp it in the upright position. Protect the floor beneath the paddle, because it is going to drip. Now take the soaked nylon cord, find the center by holding it up, and carefully place it over the edge of the paddle. You will need to squeeze the nylon a little as you guide it along the edge with your fingers, but do so gently so as not to wring out too much of the resin. Gravity helps you hold the cord in place except where the paddle tapers down to the throat. To take care of this, simply push a straight pin through the nylon into the cedar. If there is extra nylon cord, it is OK to leave a little of the nylon dangling; it has to be trimmed when cured anyway. After a half-hour or so, when the resin gets a little tacky, check the cord to be sure it is still where you want it. Corrections are easily made at this time and the resin is sticky enough so it will not move again.

As mentioned previously, the resin will run down the shaft and will have to be removed, at least most of it, later by sanding. You can minimize this by taping some plastic or wax paper just above the throat to catch this run-off and perhaps save some sanding later on.

8. Fill any voids between the cord and blade.

Because of the difficulty of working around the nylon cord, it is recommended that you allow the sealer and the soaked nylon cord to come to full cure before proceeding. After 24 hours, work can continue on the paddle blade. Remove the pins by twisting and pulling with a pair of pliers. Cut the hardened rope with a tapering cut so it makes a smooth transition to the paddle shaft (throat) or slightly below. If there are voids between the paddle and the nylon cord, they can be filled with an epoxy/silica mix. Make the mixture to a thick paste consistency and fill the voids. The color will match the nylon perfectly. You will have to wait for this mixture to cure before continuing with the sanding.

9. Sand the paddle.

Next you will need to do some sanding to remove bubbles and other irregularities from the surface of the blade, as well as to prepare it for a good mechanical bond with your fiberglass. Don't over-do the sanding; you don't want to remove the sealer coat back into the bare wood.

10. Apply any paper decoration.

If you wish to place some paper with artwork or identification under the fiberglass, now is the time. The photos on page 74 show a logo and identification applied in this manner. The logo was made on an ink-jet printer on white paper, but could be made on a photocopier or by hand on any color paper you wish. It is a good idea to experiment with the paper and markers on some scrap before applying it to your paddle. Some are not as compatible with the resin as others. Some papers almost disappear when resin is applied and the result looks like a decal. When your artwork is ready and before you proceed with the fiberglassing, spread a little resin on the spot where the paper will go and put it in place.

11. Drape and trim the fiberglass.

You are ready to start fiberglassing. The cloth will be applied one side at a time; again, gravity will be on your side. Secure the paddle in a horizontal position with the blade not touching anything. Place some plastic under the blade to prevent drips from reaching your floor. The fiberglass cloth can be scraps left over from the canoe building or a lighter weight cloth can be used to shave off a few more ounces. Cut out a piece of 6 ounce, or lighter, fiberglass cloth so that it is about 2" (51mm) larger than the blade. The cloth should reach up to, or almost to, the throat. I have used fiberglass weights from 6 ounces down to 1.5 ounces with good results.

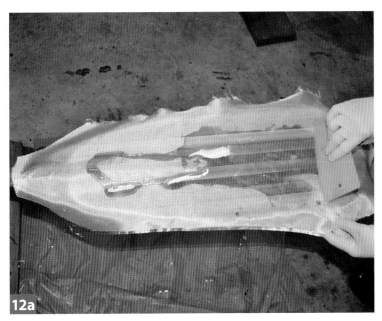

Wet out the fiberglass. Spread the resin with the squeegee and after all is wetted out remove the excess resin. Do only one side of the blade at a time.

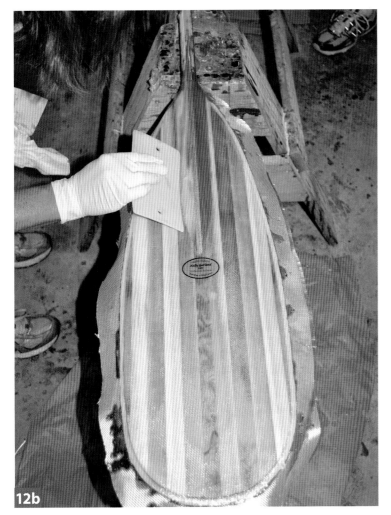

Squeegee the spine. Use the edge of the squeegee to ensure there is no bridging of the fiberglass across the valley between the spine and the blade. When this is done, leave it alone to cure. The other side is done the same way.

12. Wet out the fiberglass.

With the cloth in place, pour the remainder of the resin/hardener mix over the cloth. Use a squeegee to spread the resin until the cloth becomes transparent over the entire blade. You may have to be a little careful as you squeegee over the paper not to move it. Pay special attention to the area of the pointed end of the spine. It is easy to leave too much resin in the valley between the blade and the spine, and this allows the cloth to float up. Next, carefully squeegee out excess resin and use it to reinforce the rope edge of the paddle. The best way to do this is to use your squeegee like a snowplow, depositing the excess resin along the edges as you go along. This procedure does two things. First, it will provide resin to fill in any remaining voids or crevices that may exist between the rope and the wood edge of the paddle. Second, it weights down the cloth that extends beyond the paddle edge, ensuring good contact between the cloth and the nylon cord.

Do not try to bring the fiberglass cloth around the edge of the paddle. It will not make that sharp a bend without causing bubbles, and besides, you don't need it. You have that durable nylon rope. All you need is to ensure you have a good bond between the cloth and the rope all the way around.

13. Fill the cloth.

When properly done, the resin wets out the cloth, but does not completely fill it. So, you should be able to see the weave of the cloth and the surface will have a satin (not glossy) look. If you can't see air bubbles anywhere, especially near the edge, the fiberglassing is complete. Leave it for 24 hours, but if you can catch it in the gel stage, this is the best time to put on another thin coat of epoxy to completely fill the cloth and leave a glossy finish. If you cannot do this during the gel stage, then wait and do this fill coat after both sides of the paddle have been fiberglassed.

14. Trim the excess cloth.

The other side of the blade is done exactly like the first. If you did not trim the excess cloth at the gel stage, do so before proceeding. Trim as close as possible to the nylon rope with a sharp knife. Then take a fine wood rasp, and using lengthwise strokes, remove the remainder of the excess cloth back to, but not rasping into, the nylon rope. You will probably find you need to do some fine rasping regardless of when you did the trimming. If you deposited the excess resin near the edge, as mentioned above, there is sufficient resin in this area to achieve a nice rounded edge without rasping into the nylon. Remove any drips that may have accumulated from the previous fiberglassing, then go ahead and fiberglass the remaining side.

15. Feather the edges.

When cured, you will finish up the edge again as instructed in Step 14. At the point where the fiberglass meets wood near the throat, you should feather the fiberglass edge with a fine rasp or sandpaper until the edge cannot be felt when you run your fingers over it. Properly done, feathering makes the edge undetectable when the paddle is complete.

16. Fix any air pockets.

Check the blade, especially the edge where the nylon rope joins wood, for air pockets. If they are tiny they will do no harm, and if you can live with them, will not require further attention. If they are large, take care of them by opening them and filling with thickened resin. The closer to the tip the bubble is, the more potential for trouble, because this is where the paddle receives the most bumping and grinding.

   If the filling layer of resin was not applied during the gel stage, don't do it now—the shaft and grip will also receive a coating of waterproofing resin, and you can do it all at once.

Apply resin. When you are satisfied with the sanding of the shaft and grip, give the whole paddle a coat of epoxy resin. This will be the fill coat for the fiberglass on the blade and a sealer coat for the shaft and grip.

Apply polyurethane. Thoroughly wash the paddle with clear water, and then give the entire paddle a coat of exterior polyurethane, which has an ultra-violet filter.

17. Sand the shaft and grip.

Now is the time to finish sanding the shaft and grip. Also, give the blade a good sanding to prepare it for the final coat of resin (if it wasn't done during the gel stage). When you are satisfied with the shape, size, and smoothness of the shaft and grip, and you have sanded the blade, you are ready for a layer of resin over the entire paddle, or just the shaft and grip if the blade was previously done.

18. Apply resin.

The resin mixture can be applied with a throwaway brush. Use a generous amount so you end up with a nice glossy surface over the whole paddle—blade, shaft, and grip. You may want to do this process in two steps so you can hang the paddle to cure by a dry part, but I do it all at once. Here's how. In a floor joist overhead, I drove two 3" (76mm) drywall screws so at least two inches (51mm) protrude, and far enough apart so I could hang the wet paddle between them by the grip. There is always a little roughness where the paddle contacts the screws, but that is easily smoothed out. Hang or stand the paddle so that the resin can run off and it will smooth itself out into a nice, glossy, waterproof surface. When the coating reaches the gel state, repeat the coating if needed. Do this as many times as you feel necessary, but one coat is usually sufficient. Remember, the more resin, the heavier the paddle. If you are doing just the shaft and grip at this point, then hang the paddle with the (previously finished) blade end up.

19. Rub down the paddle with steel wool.

When the final coating of resin has cured, you are ready to apply the finishing touch, which is a coating of exterior polyurethane. The epoxy resin has to be protected from the sun's ultra-violet rays, so use an exterior polyurethane varnish with a UV filter. (Most good ones have the UV filter.) Prepare the entire paddle by giving it a good rubdown with steel wool. I use #00 steel wool for this. When finished, the surface should be rather flat or matte looking, but smooth. Now the paddle is ready for the polyurethane.

20. Wash off the paddle with water.

Once the gloss is removed from the entire paddle with steel wool, give the paddle a good washing with plenty of water. For some reason, the epoxy dust causes the polyurethane not to cure properly. So, if you don't want to end up with a sticky mess, do a good job of washing it down. Make sure the paddle is dry before proceeding.

21. Apply polyurethane.

Usually two coats of polyurethane are all that is needed to provide protection and give the paddle an attractive surface. Cosmetic maintenance in the future will require only that you sand a little and apply a little more polyurethane.

That's it; your paddle is finished! I hope you enjoyed building it, and enjoy using it even more. It will provide years of enjoyment and personal satisfaction.

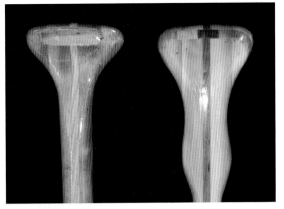

Front grip profiles. Here you can see the front profiles of the paddle grips. Make whichever one seems more comfortable to you.

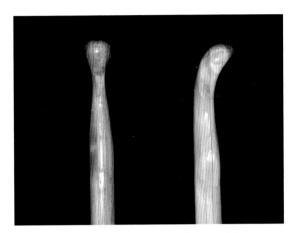

Side grip profiles. Here you can see the side views of the paddle grips.

The new paddles are complete. Jason and Kelly Garland show off their new paddles. Now they have to wait for spring to use their new canoe and paddles.

Paddle identification. Adding a label to the paddle is easily done, and will last for a long time. It will identify the paddle as belonging to you. During my years of guiding, I had several lost paddles returned because I had my name and contact information on them.

Paper labels. Here's another computer-generated label. The color does tend to fade with time, especially the reds. The canoe in this label was bright red originally.

Decorative woodburning. Be creative when adding your decorations—maps, landscape drawings, and more are possible. This paddle features a map of the Allagash Wilderness Waterway.

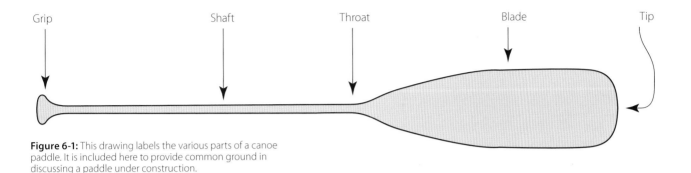

Grid   Shaft   Throat   Blade   Tip

Figure 6-1: This drawing labels the various parts of a canoe paddle. It is included here to provide common ground in discussing a paddle under construction.

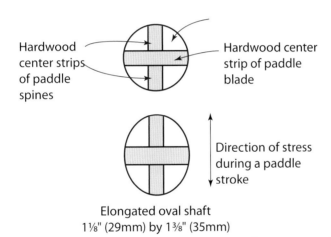

Hardwood center strips of paddle spines

Hardwood center strip of paddle blade

Direction of stress during a paddle stroke

Elongated oval shaft
1⅛" (29mm) by 1⅜" (35mm)

Figure 6-2: Shaft cross-section. This drawing represents the cross-section of the shaft of the paddles we are going to build. In order to make the paddle lightweight and strong, a combination of soft wood (cedar) and hardwood are used. The shaded cross represents the hardwood. The X formed by the hardwood provides a strong paddle shaft, yet is much lighter than if solid hardwood were used. If extra strength is desired, the oval (lower) shaft can be used.

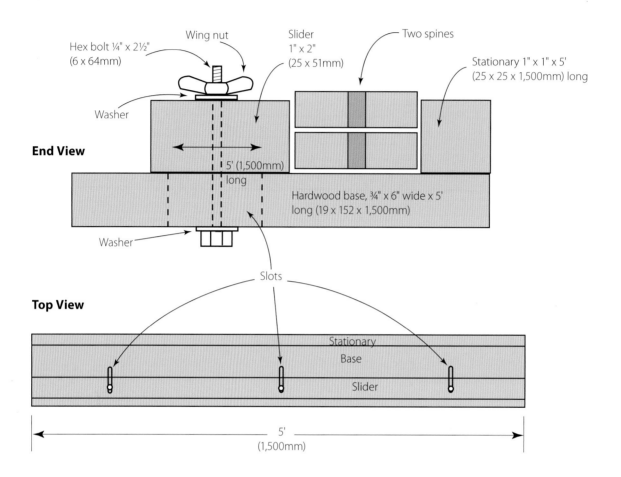

Figure 6-3: Clamping jig. This drawing is a way to make a simple clamping jig to facilitate clamping up the spines. The spine parts can be glued up without this jig, but it makes life a little easier. The bolts in the slider prevent it from tipping up and causing the spines to go out of line. It should be made to glue up the longest spines you ever expect to make.

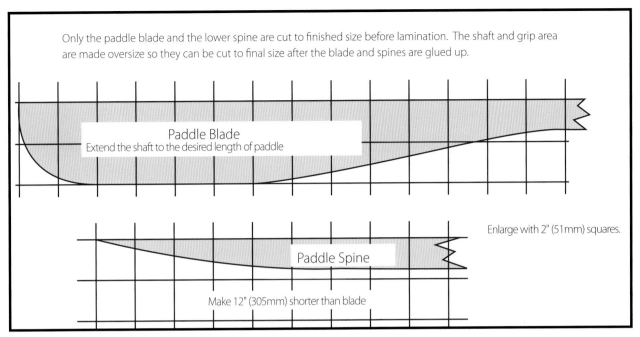

Only the paddle blade and the lower spine are cut to finished size before lamination. The shaft and grip area are made oversize so they can be cut to final size after the blade and spines are glued up.

Paddle Blade
Extend the shaft to the desired length of paddle

Paddle Spine

Enlarge with 2" (51mm) squares.

Make 12" (305mm) shorter than blade

Figure 6-4: Blade and spine pattern.

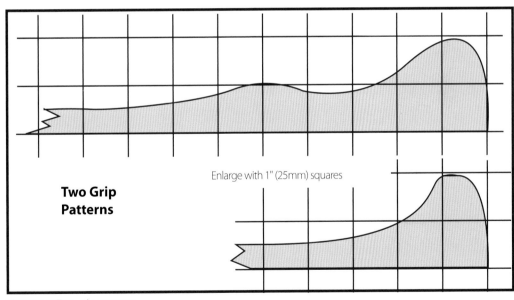

Two Grip
Patterns

Enlarge with 1" (25mm) squares

Figure 6-5: Two grip patterns.

My wife, Dot, and niece Mary Gilpatrick enjoy a game while waiting for breakfast. With the checkerboard painted on the cover of the box and checkers stowed inside, the game takes up very little room. The white box is a cooler, lined with Styrofoam. I used different colors on all my boxes to help in identifying their contents.

Chapter 7

TRIP BOX

If you plan a canoe trip or other extended outing of some kind, one of your first considerations will be provisioning the expedition—what you and others will eat. Then you face the problem of how to carry it all. Many years ago, as a young guide starting out in the canoe-tripping business, I started reading, looking around, and asking others what they used.

I soon found out there was no standard. In fact, everyone seemed to have different ideas on the subject. Luckily, before I got too confused, I decided that my ideas were as good as any. Some people took great pride that their containers were made to fit the interior of the canoe. I thought that looked nice—but those boxes don't fit the people who have to carry them, and do we really have to worry about the comfort of the canoe? It took two people to carry each of those boxes, not because of the weight, but because of the design.

My reading convinced me that tradition was the strongest reason that certain types of containers were used. In the northeast, the pack basket is the traditional receptacle for transporting food and gear on canoe expeditions. In the Midwest, the Duluth

Materials (for 2 boxes)

- Epoxy resin and hardener
- 2 or 3 disposable brushes
- 1 roller cover
- (1) 4' x 8' (1,220 x 2,440mm) sheet of ¼" (6mm) plywood
- 1 quart of paint
- Hot glue sticks (optional)
- 1 pack of ¾" (19mm) brads or ⁹⁄₁₆" (14mm) staples
- 1 pack of ³⁄₁₆" (21mm) staples
- Sandpaper, 1 sheet 50-grit and 2 sheets 80-grit
- 2 pieces 6-ounce fiberglass cloth, approximately 20" x 60" (508 x 1,524mm)
- 2 pieces 6-ounce fiberglass cloth, approximately 10" x 24" (254 x 610mm)
- 2 pieces 6-ounce fiberglass cloth, approximately 18" x 22" (457 x 559mm)
- 1 squeegee
- 4 pieces hardwood, ½' x 4" x 15" (13 x 102 x 381mm)
- 52 rivets or stove bolts and nuts, 1" (25mm) long
- 4' (1,220mm) webbing to make lifting straps (you could use discarded auto seat belts)
- 4 cover latches
- 4 pieces hardwood ⅜" x 3" x 3" (10 x 76 x 76mm)
- 2 sets shoulder straps (see "Resources and Supplies")
- 1 package gasket material (ours was tubular vinyl gasket)
- Additional items to make one cooler
- 2' (610mm) hardwood, ¾" x ¾" (19 x 19mm)
- 1 sheet of builder's Styrofoam, 2' x 8' (610 x 2,440mm)
- Approximately 10 square feet of 6-ounce fiberglass cloth
- 1 pack of gasket material

Tools

- Table saw or circular hand saw
- Hand saw
- Carpenter's rule
- Hot glue gun (optional)
- Stapler
- 4-in-1 rasp
- Sander (optional)
- Roller frame
- Scissors
- Electric hand drill
- ³⁄₁₆" (5mm) drill bit (may need larger)

pack was the pack of choice for the traditionalist. Both types of packs had too many drawbacks to satisfy me.

None of the trip boxes I saw were waterproof. In fact, most were not even rainproof, which meant they had to be protected in wet weather. Other than carrying provisions, the boxes had no function. Early on I learned the more uses you can find for any item you carry, the more valuable and worthy of its space and weight that item is.

So I set out to design my own containers. They had to:
• Be backpackable, leaving the traveler's hands free to carry smaller items on each portage. (Fit the people instead of the canoe).
• Be rainproof—preferably waterproof—so they could be left outside. (Leaving the dry spaces for people instead of gear.)
• Serve purposes other than just carrying provisions.
• Afford some protection from scavenging animals.
• Be tough enough to stand up to year-in, year-out handling by people who did not own them. (Ask anyone who rents out equipment about this phenomenon.)

The only thing I liked about our traditional Maine pack basket was its size. So I designed the boxes with roughly the same capacity as a large Maine pack basket—nearly 4,000 cubic inches (100,000 cubic mm).

At the risk of breaking my arm by patting myself on the back, I can say the boxes I came up with met my expectations and in some cases exceeded them. Their weight and design make one a reasonable load for the average person for most portages.

Fiberglassed and with a lid like that of a shoebox, the boxes are automatically rainproof. I add gaskets to help protect the contents in the event of an upset. The boxes with gaskets have come through a number of upsets, and not one has resulted in a box taking in more than a cup of water or losing a significant amount of food. Many times they came through completely dry; it depends on how long the cover is held under before the box floats free and rights itself. Emptying the boxes as soon as possible after an upset minimizes the damage done by even a cup of water.

I saw the possibility of using them for seats, and that the cover could become a checkerboard. Necessity mothered other uses. They are good to tie tarp ropes

Midway through a portage, Ross Mosher demonstrates that carrying a box on your back leaves the hands free to carry all those miscellaneous items that don't seem to fit any other place. I used to pad the boxes with foam for back comfort, but discovered that they are not all that uncomfortable to carry as is. although not designed to be carried all day as backpackers do with theirs, for a mile or two they are okay.

onto, eliminating the need for cutting and driving stakes into the ground. They make handy stepstools. Placed in a row, they make a nice serving line to feed a large group, or provide a windbreak around a campfire or camp stove. And, as food is consumed, they provide a dry spot to store other items.

I make no guarantees regarding protection from animals, but the following story is interesting and true.

I made a pair of these packs for our friends, Hatherly and Alice Souther, and they went on a trip on Allagash stream in northern Maine. Early one morning, a commotion in the kitchen area of their campsite awakened them. They looked out and saw a full-grown black bear tearing, biting, swatting, and generally mauling their food pack. Finally he gave up and plunked the pack into the cold fireplace, obviously chagrined at not gaining entry into the pack.

The Southers still have the pack. We replaced one ripped strap handle and rebolted one shoulder strap. The tooth marks in the fiberglass are still there. To the Southers, they are trophies of a memorable experience; to me, they are a testimony to the durability of the packs.

I am still using only my second set of boxes. The first are still serviceable, replaced only because I wanted to make improvements (reflected in this chapter). These boxes will last the average outdoor person a lifetime.

Making a Box

1. Cut the wood parts.

Fiberglass and epoxy make these food boxes tough and durable, but they need a base. To make one, buy a sheet of ¼" (6mm) plywood and cut out the parts according to the cutting guide in **Figure 7-1**. You will be able to get two boxes from each 4' x 8' (1,220 x 2,440mm) sheet, with a little left over. Or, if you happen to have a lot of paneling scraps on hand from a household project, use it and save yourself the price of the plywood. Most paneling is smooth and glossy on the exposed surface, so I recommend

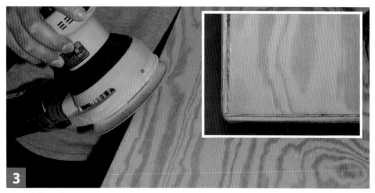

Cut the wood parts. Jason and Kelly prepare to cut the plywood on a table saw.

Glue the box.

Round the edges. Jason uses coarse (60-grit) sandpaper in a random orbit-sander. No further sanding is needed.

you put the unfinished wrong-side out, as it makes a better surface to fiberglass. Anyway, you should paint the outside for ultraviolet protection, so looks will not be a factor.

A good table saw with a large table surface is ideal for cutting out the plywood parts, but other saws, such as a hand-held circular saw, will also work. If you use a hand-held saw, I recommend clamping on a straightedge as a guide. The more accurate you are in cutting out the parts, the more easily they will go together.

2. Assemble the box.

The parts of the boxes have to be held together only well enough for you to do a little sanding and then get the fiberglass on them. After that, the fiberglass will hold everything together through decades of service. Start by making sure the parts fit together okay. A look at the measurements in **Figure 7-1** makes it obvious how the butt joints are to go together. Also, look at photo 3 inset to see the joinery. There are a number of ways to hold the butt joints in place. If you can work quickly, a hot glue gun is all you need. Spread the hot glue along the plywood edge and quickly lay the other part in place. If you make a mistake, it isn't too hard to remove the glue and try again.

Another option is using carpenter's glue and small brads or a staple gun to hold the parts in place. If you do, remove the staples or brads when the glue is dry—they would interfere with the fiberglassing— and handle the box carefully afterward because glue does not hold as well to plywood edges as it does with other surfaces.

3. Round the corners and edges.

Make sure the glue is dry and all staples or brads have been removed. Then, round all corners and edges except the openings with a sander or fine rasp. The plywood surface is already smooth enough, so you have only to concern yourself with the joints, which are now the corners and edges of your box. Rounding is important because the fiberglass cloth does not make sharp corners very well. Giving the corners a nice radius will make it easy to do a nice job of fiberglassing. The openings (top of the open box and bottom of the cover) should remain flat and square, not rounded over, as they will receive a coating of resin instead of being fiberglassed.

Fiberglassing a Box

Before you start fiberglassing, be sure to look over the general instructions in the epoxy chapter. The paragraphs that follow assume you are familiar with those instructions.

4. Seal the wood.

Like almost all other fiberglassing projects, the first step is sealing the wood with epoxy resin. A roller is the fastest way to do this but, if you don't have one, a brush will work. The important thing is getting a good layer of resin onto the wood to prepare it for the next step. If you have time to proceed with the fiberglassing as soon as the sealer reaches the gel state, do so. If you have to allow the sealer to go to final cure before proceeding, be sure to sand the surface to prepare it for the next step.

At some point you should also seal the inside of both the box and the cover. This prevents the wood from reacting to sudden changes in humidity and if something spills or water ever gets inside the box. You can do it now or later on—both methods work.

5. Apply the cloth to the box and wet it out.

Use three pieces. The first, and largest, will cover the bottom and the front and back of the box. Cut this piece approximately 20" x 60" (510 x 1,520mm). The cloth that still looks white in the photo will be moistened and brought around the ends as far as it will reach—2" (50mm) is about right. At the corners, cut a slit in the cloth so it can overlap itself. That will keep the job neat. (See: Reinforcing Corners for Fiberglassing.)

We placed the box on a makeshift pedestal so the top of the box (at the bottom in the photos) would not have to rest on anything. This made it possible for the cloth to just hang beyond the top, as it should. The photo also shows the use of a foam brush for resin. That works, but unless you work quickly, you will probably use more than one foam brush, so it might be more economical to use one throwaway chip brush. You could also use a roller for this purpose. After you wet out the cloth, go over it with a squeegee.

When the bottom, front, and back are covered and the cloth neatly brought around, you can apply the cloth to the sides. Use two pieces of cloth cut to approximately 10" x 24" (254 x 610mm). This cloth should overlap the cloth you brought around from

Seal the wood. Jason uses a roller, which gets the job done quickly.

Apply the first piece of fiberglass cloth. Put one sheet over the sides and top of the box. Leave about a 2" (51mm) overhang on each side to be brought around to the end of the box as shown. (The fiberglass shown is 6-ounce.)

Adjust the overhang. Bring the overhang around the corner to the end; a brush is the best tool for this job. Cut a slit in the overhang at the corners to ensure that it lays flat.

Apply the second piece of fiberglass cloth. Apply fiberglass to the end of the box so it overlaps the overhang that was brought around and sticks to the wet resin already there. All that is left is to wet it out.

the front and back by an inch or so. You will need to be a little careful in wetting out and squeegeeing these pieces because you don't want to disturb the cloth you applied previously.

When the box is covered, go on and fiberglass the cover using one piece of cloth approximately 18" x 22" (457 x 559mm). Bring the cloth over the edge and down over the sides letting it hang beyond the cover opening as you did with the top of the box. At the corners you will slit the cloth and overlap the flaps so they lay down nice and neat.

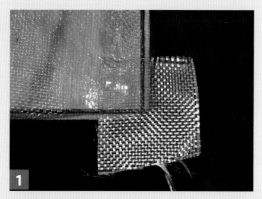

Cut the patch. Make each about 1 ½" (38mm) square.

Place and wet out the patch. Gloved fingers are the best tools for getting the patch to behave. When it's positioned correctly, wet it out thoroughly.

Apply a final coat of resin. This helps smooth things out.

Adjust the patch. Manipulate it as needed.

Reinforcing Corners for Fiberglassing

One of the challenges in fiberglassing is completely covering the corners. No matter how carefully you cut and fit the pieces you bring around the corners, there seems to always be a spot that the glass fibers do not cover. Because the corners of a box are usually the most vulnerable to damage, it is important that they be well reinforced. The following is the best solution I have found. I recommend doing it on all four corners of both the box and its cover while the fiberglass is still wet.

Cut a small square of cloth about 1 ½" x 1 ½" (38 x 38mm). At this size, the cloth has enough give that it will lay down and completely cover the corner without having to be cut. After final cure, do a little feathering of the edges with 80-grit sandpaper, and the corner will look great and be well protected.

Finishing a Box

6. When the resin reaches the gel stage, trim the cloth.

This is a good time to trim the cloth around the top of the box and the bottom of the cover. Trim it flush with the plywood edge.

7. Follow the fiberglassing process as shown in the epoxy chapter.

If possible, apply the weave-filling resin coat as soon as the resin in your fiberglass reaches the gel stage. You can feather out those fiberglass edges when you sand the rest of the box in preparation for a coat of paint or varnish. If you cannot do the filler at the gel stage, sand thoroughly before you do it.

8. Seal the inside of the box and cover with resin if you have not already.

Be sure the exposed edges of plywood at the top of the box and the bottom of the cover are completely sealed with resin as well.

Paint the box. It's a good idea to wait until you have all the wooden parts in place before you do this.

9. Sand as desired.

How much cosmetic sanding you do to the outside of the box is a matter of personal preference. Some places will have multiple layers of fiberglass because of the necessity of overlapping. These areas will show up when a glossy finish such as paint or polyurethane varnish is applied. Utility requires only that you feather out the exposed edges of the overlapping cloth, but if you wish to carry the sanding further to obtain a fairer surface, that is up to you. However, do be aware the boxes are made for rugged outdoor travel, and before long yours will probably look like the old veteran in the photo on page 79.

10. Paint the box.

(If you intend to add skids or other wooden attachments, as shown on page 84, it is a good idea to wait until those are on the box before you paint.) Paint is a good idea, for two reasons. First, plywood usually has nothing to offer in the way of beautiful wood. If you do want the wood to show through, use a good polyurethane varnish with a UV filter to protect the resin. Most modern polyurethanes contain UV filters. Second, epoxy resin does not like the ultraviolet rays of the sun.

Most any good-quality enamel will work well if you prepare the surface properly by removing any amine blush and giving the surface a thorough sanding. Be sure to wash off the sanding dust with water before applying paint or polyurethane.

I used a color-coding system to organize my boxes. For example, on trips with a large party (up to 12 people), I took three food boxes: breakfast items were in the lightest-colored box, lunches in the medium-shade one, and supper meals in the darkest-colored box.

CHAPTER 7: TRIP BOX

Adding to a Box

The photo at right shows all of the attachments to the box. If yours is for a special purpose, you may want to modify some of them. Otherwise, follow along in this section and mount them as pictured.

11. Add skids to the bottom of the box.

Your boxes are going to see years of hard abuse. They will be dragged over rocks, slid through mud, dropped, and subjected to many other indignities. The bottom will receive the brunt of the abrasion from the ground, but adding hardwood skids gives it some protection. Skids also provide a point for the lower attachment of the shoulder straps.

Figure 7-2 shows how the skids should be located at the base of the box, extending about ½" (13mm) below the bottom of the box. It is a good idea to finish the skids before attaching them to your box so there is some finish on the inside of the skid (between the box and the skid). Water will seep in there, and finish will make the wood less likely to warp or rot.

Attach the skids with countersunk flatheaded stove bolts or rivets. If you use bolts, it is better to have the nuts and the ends of the bolts on the outside of the box, where you can trim the end of the bolt flush with the nut, than to have them sticking out inside the box, where they can puncture food packages and do other mischief. You can even counterbore for the nuts, if you wish, so they will be even more unobtrusive.

12. Attach nylon straps.

The nylon straps on each side of the boxes are there for moving the box around and for short hauls when you don't want to bother putting it on your back. I put them about 12" (305mm) up from the bottom and use enough loop to allow a hand to grip them comfortably. A word of caution: when two people cooperate to carry the box by these handles, the backs of their hands will be ground into the latches. Avoid this by simply holding it the other way, so the palm faces the box. You could try to mount the straps lower; I did. But then they are so low that, at times at least, the box is top-heavy. I fussed with the

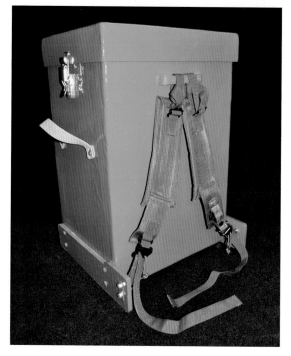

The completed box with everything attached. I used flathead machine bolts to attach everything to the box, as the wood is not thick enough to use wood screws. I countersunk the flatheads on the inside to keep them from tearing anything in the box.

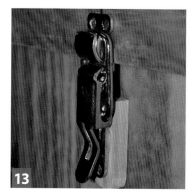

Mount the latches.

problem for a long time and finally decided it was easiest to simply turn the hand.

Like the skids, the straps can be attached to the box with rivets or stove bolts. If you use bolts, keep the flatheads on the inside and the nuts on the outside. These boxes are designed to protect the contents, not to look pretty.

13. Mount latches.

Use two, one on each side of the box. Center and align them carefully. Put a piece of wood under the lower part of the latch to bring it out flush with the shoebox-type cover. A thickness of ⅜" (10mm) worked best for me, but measure yours to be sure. I use a bit of hot glue between the metal and the wood of the bottom part. This holds the wood and metal together and makes locating and fastening them a lot easier.

Install the latches with no tension—so they do not pull down on the cover with any force. That way when you put the gasket inside the cover later on, the latch will pull the cover hard enough to compress the gasket and give you a good seal. If you give it tension with no gasket there, you may not be able to close it when you do have one. I have found that even when I am extremely careful to center the latches and make their tensions as identical as possible, they still don't work well interchangeably. So, once you have everything finished, mark the cover and box so you can put it back on the same way every time. I use identification labels for this purpose.

Install the gasket. That is tubular vinyl gasket inside the cover.

14. Add shoulder straps.

The design of your shoulder straps will dictate how you mount them. For these, I used a slotted piece of hardwood at the top and a small U-bolt at the bottom.

When I first thought of these boxes, I envisioned a strap or pad at the base of the box between the extensions of the skids. In fact, that is what the extension was originally there for; it has remained because it is a good place to attach the shoulder straps. As it turned out, however, the box does not dig or gouge into the back in any way, so those straps or pads are unnecessary. That isn't to say that you would want to backpack this box for hours on end—it isn't designed for that. But for portaging for a mile or two, it is perfectly comfortable.

15. Install the cover gasket.

I have tried everything the hardware stores have to offer, and tubular vinyl gasket is the best and easiest to use that I have found. It is the stuff used to seal around doors and places like that. It has a cross-section shaped like a tadpole—just staple or glue it into place with the "tadpole's" tail. I have also used foam material that is made to seal around windows, etc.

This battle-scarred veteran is far more efficient than any commercial cooler I ever tried, and one person can carry it. Built like the food boxes, it is insulated with two 1" (25mm) sheets of construction-grade Styrofoam (available at home centers and lumber yards), then fiberglassed inside to protect the insulation. The gasket inside the cover is the thin foam material used between house foundations and the sill. The insulation means the strap attachments had to be constructed so the straps could be replaced if necessary.

Making a Cooler

You can buy coolers of all shapes and sizes, so why make your own? The answer is for durability, ease of handling, and food-holding qualities. On weeklong midsummer canoe trips, these coolers keep food fresh right up to the last day, so you can eat pretty much the same foods as you do at home. This doesn't seem like much of a luxury until you have to do without it for an extended period of time. Spend a week, or even less, eating nothing but freeze-dried meals or other fare prepared with non-perishable ingredients, and you will know what I mean.

For best results, pack the cooler with unfrozen food in reverse order (so the first day's meal is on top, etc.), then put the whole thing in a freezer and let it all freeze solid. Packing the food while unfrozen saves a lot of space and gives you a solid frozen mass that will hold longer than it would otherwise. However, doing this requires a rather large chest freezer to accomplish this. For my larger cooler, I load a plywood box insert with food the same way and place that in the freezer. It doesn't take as much space as putting the cooler itself in the freezer would. On the day I depart, I simply pull it out of the freezer and put it in the cooler. You could do the same with the standard-size cooler if need be. The basic box for these coolers is the same shown earlier in this chapter through the fiberglassing stage except for the following modifications.

1. Fasten straps and carrying handles to wood attachments, not directly to box.

See photo on page 85. Insulation will cover the inside of the box, which would be a problem if you needed to repair or replace a strap or handle that was attached as shown on the regular trip boxes.

2. Install insulation.

With insulation in place you will have about 1,600 cubic inches (40,000 cubic mm) of space in the standard-size box . If you need more space than that, increase the size of the box. For large groups I use a box that provides 4,000 cubic inches (100,000mm) of interior space. With it I can provision a group of 12 people with fresh food for a seven-day river trip. For smaller groups, or shorter trips, I use the box shown in the photo on page 85.

Foam insulation is usually available in 2' x 8' (610 x 2,440mm) and 4' x 8' (1,220 x 2,440mm) sheets from a local lumberyard or home center in 1" (25mm) and 2" (51mm) thicknesses. The box shown has two layers of 1" (25mm) Styrofoam, but either thickness is okay. I like the thinner material so I can make overlapping joints at the corners, but that may be nitpicking. At any rate, you need 2" (51mm) of foam insulation on the bottom, all four sides, and in the cover. One 2' x 8' (610 x 2,440mm) piece of 2" (51mm) foam will do one box.

3. Carefully fit the insulation in place.

Do the cover as shown on page 85. Take care to place the cover insulation so it fits into the cavity created by the box insulation, but allow enough clearance to fiberglass it as you did the box insulation. Because of the large bearing surface, a variety of materials would work for the cover gasket. The one shown is plastic foam—what builders put between the top of a concrete foundation and the wooden sill of the building. Builders generally have spare pieces of it; if you don't know one, you'll probably have to buy a 100' (30,500mm) roll...which means you'll probably want to look for something else.

4. Fiberglass the box and cover interiors.

The foam doesn't need to be sealed, so the first step in the process is wetting out the fiberglass cloth. It is fussy work because of the limited space, but if you proceed carefully and methodically it will come out fine.

Do the bottom and each of the sides with separate pieces of cloth, overlapping each for a good seal. At the top, bring the fiberglass cloth up over the top of the insulation and out over the edge of the plywood top of the box. Be sure to round off the outer edge of the plywood to allow the fiberglass to go around it smoothly. Keep the top of the box as smooth as possible to allow a good seal with the cover.

Notice the X on the cover and the box in the photo on page 85. It is there to ensure the cover is placed in the same position each time it is closed. This provides for the best possible fit and seal.

5. Sand.

When the resin has fully cured, use 80-grit sandpaper to feather out all the edges where the fiberglass cloth overlapped. Then give the whole thing a good sanding to prepare it for the filler coats of resin.

6. Apply resin.

Use as many filler coats as you deem necessary, but one is probably sufficient.

Making a Pantry Box

Another kind of box that I regularly use is my pantry, or kitchen, box. I try to stay flexible and make changes when needed and when something better comes along. The box shown is about 20" (508mm) wide, 30" (762mm) long, and 8" (203mm) deep, with a 6" (152mm)-deep cover so it can adjust to changing loads. Straps over the top hold it in place. It is constructed in the same manner as a regular trip box, but without a gasket.

Size the pantry box to fit your needs. For a couple or a small family, this box may be enough all by itself, eliminating the need for a food box. Without the gasket it is not waterproof—but it is rainproof, and does not take up dry people space during wet weather. I like to use skids and attach shoulder straps (not shown in the picture) to the bottom of the box.

Allagash Muffins

These muffins provide an easy way to have fresh "bread" when there is no oven available. See the Canoe Country Bread recipe on page 23 for the mix. Eat Allagash Muffins hot with butter, jelly, sugar-cinnamon mix, or whatever you have on hand that sounds good.

4 cups of Canoe Country Bread dry mix

¼ cup flour

Carefully add small amounts of water to the bread mix until the dough is quite stiff. Using flour to keep the dough from sticking, make patties about the size of English muffins and about ½" (13mm) thick. If you don't have extra flour with you, just save a little of the bread mix before adding the water, and use that. Cook the muffins on a griddle, skillet, grill, or anything else you can get hot. They are probably the best cooked on a forked stick over the hot coals of a campfire.

This kitchen box, which is approximately 20" x 30" x 8" (508 x 762 x 203mm), holds everything I need to prepare meals on the river except food. The cover is 6" (152mm) deep, constructed shoebox-style to adjust up or down depending on the load being carried. The box also has shoulder straps on the bottom between the skids. It's a heavy load, but it beats tying up two people to transport it. The adjustable cover prohibits installing a gasket, so I always carried it in my canoe, and in more than 30 years it never got dunked. A similar box held my tools—tarps, saws, an axe, and all the other items that didn't fit in anywhere else.

Start by ripping the 4' x 8' (1,220 x 2,440mm) plywood into 5 strips

2¾" (70mm)

← 15¾" (400mm) → ← 15½" (394mm) → ← 12" (305mm) →

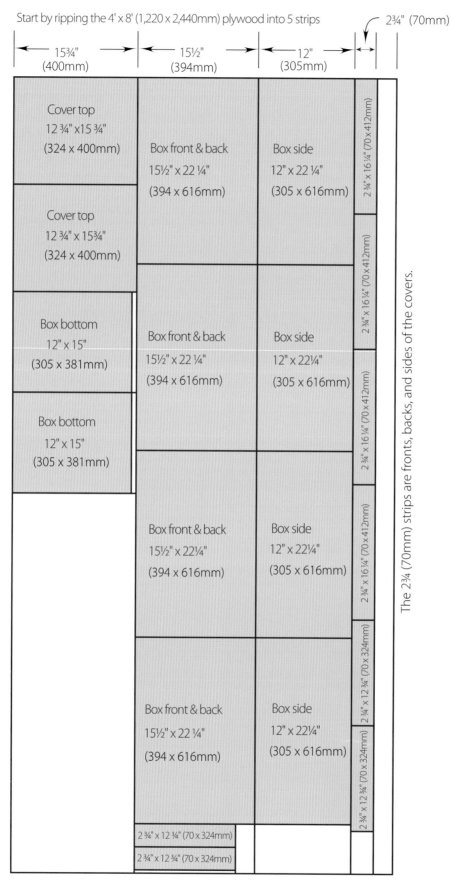

Cover top
12 ¾" x15 ¾"
(324 x 400mm)

Cover top
12 ¾" x 15¾"
(324 x 400mm)

Box bottom
12" x 15"
(305 x 381mm)

Box bottom
12" x 15"
(305 x 381mm)

Box front & back
15½" x 22 ¼"
(394 x 616mm)

Box front & back
15½" x 22 ¼"
(394 x 616mm)

Box front & back
15½" x 22¼"
(394 x 616mm)

Box front & back
15½" x 22 ¼"
(394 x 616mm)

Box side
12" x 22 ¼"
(305 x 616mm)

Box side
12" x 22¼"
(305 x 616mm)

Box side
12" x 22¼"
(305 x 616mm)

Box side
12" x 22¼"
(305 x 616mm)

2 ¾" x 16 ¼" (70 x 412mm)

2 ¾" x 16 ¼" (70 x 412mm)

2 ¾" x 16 ¼" (70 x 412mm)

2 ¾" x 16 ¼" (70 x 412mm)

2 ¾" x 12 ¾" (70 x 324mm)

2 ¾" x 12 ¾" (70 x 324mm)

The 2¾ (70mm) strips are fronts, backs, and sides of the covers.

2 ¾" x 12 ¾" (70 x 324mm)

2 ¾" x 12 ¾" (70 x 324mm)

Figure 7-1: Cutting diagram. You can get two complete trip
boxes from one sheet of ¼" (6mm) plywood with a little left over.

Kitchen Box Packing Checklists

• Pantry Box

- Cook set, cups, plates, etc.
- Silverware
- Big spoon
- Spatula
- Grill
- Griddle
- Reflector oven
- Reflector oven pan
- Bread and cake pans
- Gas stove
- Water pails
- Coffee pot
- Leather gloves
- Water filter
- Extra matches
- Hand soap
- Paper towels
- Vegetable oil
- Coffee
- Creamer
- Sugar
- Tea
- Clorox
- Cinnamon sugar
- Pepper
- Salt
- Flour
- Jelly
- Nonstick spray
- Tablecloth
- Hand sanitizer
- (Other) _____

• Tool Box

- Folding saw
- Chain saw
- Gas and oil (chain saw)
- Axe
- Shovel
- Tarps (2)
- Ropes
- Toilet paper
- Dishpan
- Sponge
- Dish detergent
- Scouring pads
- Bug repellent
- Medical kit
- Stove oven
- Canoe repair tape
- Extra plastic bags
- Fire pot
- Games
- Extra saw blades
- Extra tent pegs
- Tent plastic
- (Other)

_____

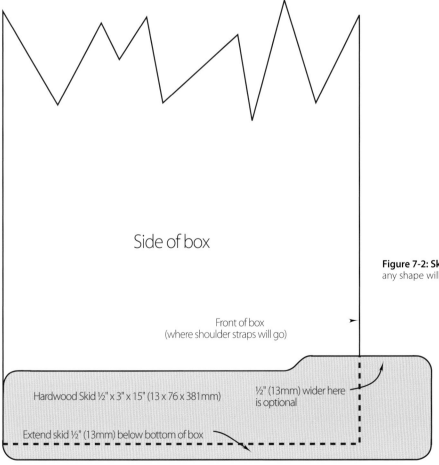

Side of box

Front of box
(where shoulder straps will go)

Hardwood Skid ½" x 3" x 15" (13 x 76 x 381mm)

½" (13mm) wider here
is optional

Extend skid ½" (13mm) below bottom of box

Figure 7-2: Skid location. The shape shown is a suggestion—any shape will do as long as it serves its purpose.

Materials

- Hardwood boards long enough to make the desired mount (or plywood)
- Wood for splash guard form, 2" x 6" x 10" (51 x 152 x 254mm)
- Epoxy resin and hardener
- Cotton fibers
- Small amount of fiberglass cloth
- 6 or 8 flathead wood screws, #8, 1 ½" (38mm) long
- Dowel, ¾" (19mm), 3" or 4" (76 or 102mm) long
- Carriage bolt, ½" (13mm), long enough for your mount
- Wing nut, ½" (13mm)
- Washer, ½" (13mm)
- Sandpaper, 60 and 80 grit

Tools

- Table saw
- Band saw
- Sander
- 3 or 4 clamps
- Electric or cordless drill
- ⅝" (16mm) drill bit
- Drill bits to pre-drill for wood screws

My old 4 HP Evinrude mounted on the side of a canoe. The piece of rope between the motor and the canoe has a clip on the end; I attach it to a ring on the inside of the canoe (seat) for safety, in case the motor ever comes loose for some reason. It has never happened.

Chapter 8

CANOE MOTOR MOUNT

It has been my unhappy experience that anything sold as "universal" or "fits all" actually fits nothing. It certainly applies to mounting a motor on a canoe; I have concluded that they must be custom-made for the canoe upon which they are to be used. Here is what I have learned in years of building motor mounts, improving them, and giving them hard use.

The purist looks at a motor canoe as an abomination, but from a practical standpoint a motor canoe makes a lot of sense. I too hate to clutter up the beautiful lines of a canoe with a motor and mount; that is why I designed my mount to attach and detach easily. Just tighten the wing nut and the mount is in place. Thanks to the wing

nut, taking it off is just as easy, requiring no tools. This way I can hide the motor on the bottom of my canoe until it is needed, but still have it in place in less than a minute if need be. In my guiding business I considered the motor an insurance policy to be cashed in case of trouble—injury, contrary weather, or whatever. A big advantage of traveling by canoe is being able to float in very shallow water. When you mount a motor on your canoe you give up a little of this ability, but not much.

Because this is to be a custom job, you won't find many exact dimensions in these instructions. What you will find is how to figure what you will need for your canoe.

Laminating a Mount

Early on I learned that hardwood, even the best and strongest hardwood, splits under the continuous stress of hard use. So, again, I turned to epoxy technology, laminating the wood parts to ensure they had the endurance I required. The motor bar is 1¾" (44mm) thick, with the grain of the ¾" (19mm) center layer running at about a 30° angle to the grain of the two ½" (13mm) outer layers. You should use the angle that gives maximum strength through the notched and stepped area where the motor bar connects to the base; Motor Photo 8 shows that this could be a weak spot. For all the other wood parts, including the base, the sub-base, and even the blocks on the end of the base, I laminated the center layer at 90° to the two outer layers. You can see the laminations in the photos.

If you intend to laminate your mount, make the motor bar 1 ½" to 1 ¾" (38 to 44mm) thick, at least 24" (610mm) long, and 5" (127mm) or more wide. Make the base ¾" (19mm) thick (three ¼" [6mm] layers), at least 6" (152mm) wide, and long enough to span the canoe where you will mount it, plus 3" or 4" (76 or 102mm). The sub-base can be ¾" (19mm) thick, 4" (102mm) wide, and long enough to fit underneath the gunwales. For glue use epoxy mixed with cotton fibers; the mixture can be thin because little or no gap filling will be needed.

An alternative to laminating hardwood might be to use ¾" (19mm) plywood, which is strong enough for moderate use. To do that, just glue two pieces of plywood together to get thickness enough for the motor bar, and use the rest as is. I would not recommend using plywood if it were not for the great waterproofing ability of epoxy. When you have the plywood mount completed, fill all voids in the plywood edges and then give the whole thing a couple of coats of epoxy to protect it from moisture.

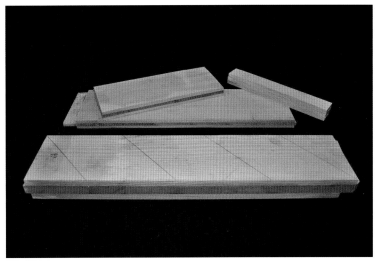

If you plan to laminate your motor mount parts, set them up this way. The motor bar blank in the foreground has the grain of the inner layer (¾" [19mm]) running at about a 30° angle to the grain of the two outer layers (½" [13mm] each). The diagonal lines indicate this angle. On the other parts the grain of the inner layer (¼" [6mm]) runs at 90° to the grain of the two outer layers (¼" [6mm] each). The narrow piece in the right rear of the photo will make the hard wood wing nut.

Making a Mount

1. Determine the working depth of the propeller.

In other words, figure out how low the propeller must be to avoid hitting the bottom of the canoe. The top of the propeller should be roughly even with the bottom of the canoe. Then use that information to determine how much (if at all) you need to drop or raise the motor in relation to the canoe gunwales. The motor bar and left side end block must, in turn, extend low or high enough to land the motor at the correct depth. (See opening photo on page 90, left end block is on right side of photo.) For the mount in the illustrations, and probably most mounts, a motor bar height of 5" (127mm) is sufficient. That means the left end block should extend down 2½" (64mm).

Determine the working depth of the propeller.

2. Cut and assemble the base, sub-base, and end blocks.

As I have mentioned, the exact dimensions depend on the size and shape of your canoe and motor. The mount should go just to the rear of the stern seat so you can sit comfortably, with your back possibly just touching the mount. The base and end blocks need to fit snugly over the top and sides of the gunwales, and the sub-base needs to fit snugly against the underside of the gunwales.

A motor running on the side of a canoe stresses the mount vertically and horizontally, and photo 2 shows how this mount addresses those stresses. The sub-base keeps the mount from twisting up and down, and the end blocks keep the mount from twisting horizontally.

Use screws and epoxy glue to attach the ¾" (19mm)-thick end blocks to the base. The right block (on left side of photo 2) only needs to be ¾" or 1" (19 or 25mm) long, but as discussed in step 1, the left block (on right side of photo) should extend down 2 ½" (64mm). If you make the blank for the base long enough, you can make the left side block from what is cut from the base blank.

From here on I will refer to the base, sub-base, and end blocks collectively as the base.

3. Clamp the base to the canoe.

Place the mount so if the motor were attached, it would be to your left and just slightly behind you. That placement means you won't have to twist around in your seat to control the motor—an important consideration if you use it for an extended period of time.

4. Determine the motor bar angle.

Make sure the canoe is sitting level. Clamp a carpenter's level to the base and make it plumb, then use a protractor of some kind to measure the vertical angle of the level, which is the same as the vertical angle of the base. In this case, that is 8°—a slight forward tilt. Most small boats and canoes have a similar tilt, and motors are built to accommodate that. The angle of the motor bar should be 10° more than the angle of the base. In this case, that makes the motor bar angle 18°.

Cut and assemble the base, sub-base, and end blocks.

Clamp the base to the canoe.

Determine the motor bar angle.

5. Cut the motor bar.

Use the height determined in step 1 and the angle determined in step 4. We did this one on a band saw with the table angled at 18°. Make it long enough to extend 10" (254mm) out over the side and about two-thirds of the way over the base. Look at the photo on page 94 to see the shape of ours. It should fit snugly against both the top and left side of the base, with the angle tilting the top toward the stern and the bottom toward the bow.

6. Drill through the motor bar and base.

Be sure everything is properly assembled and clamped before you start. Drill through everything at once to assure alignment. I recommend drilling a ⅝" (16mm) hole and then using a ½" (13mm) carriage bolt of whatever length your mount requires. The bolt should stick up about an inch above the mount.

7. Make and attach a wing nut.

Option A: Metal wing nut. If you are handy with a welder or know someone who is, weld a couple of bars to an ordinary ½" (13mm) nut. While you are at it, weld a ½" (13mm) washer to the bottom of the nut to give more surface to wind down against the wooden mount.

Option B: Hardwood wing nut. Use **Figure 8-1** and a strong piece of hardwood, preferably laminated, about 1" x 8" x 2" (25 x 203 x 51mm). Inlet an ordinary ½" (13mm) wing nut into the center edge of the wood stock. Then drill a ⅝" (16mm) hole for the bolt to extend through. Fit the wing nut into the wood, scratch it up a little with a file or grinder so the epoxy can grasp it, and epoxy it into the slot. Epoxy mixed with cotton fibers will probably do the job, but you could also use the West System 404 High-Density filler mixed with epoxy, which is especially made for hardware bonding. The bolt should be on the wing nut when you glue it in place so you can be sure the hole remains open. Wax the bolt threads with a paste wax to be sure it will release from any epoxy that might touch it. It is a good idea to remove the bolt once the epoxy has reached the gel stage; it will come out a lot easier. If any epoxy glue squeezes out on the threads, you can drill it away later, leaving only the threads of the metal wing nut.

Drill the bolt hole. When you install the carriage bolt, place a small amount of epoxy glue in the hole in the sub-base to attach the bolt to it firmly and permanently. This helps keep things together and prevent losing the bolt in a place where no replacement is possible.

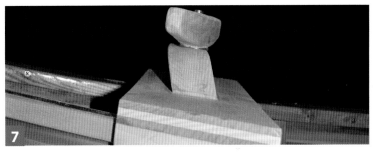

Make and attach a wing nut. This end view of the base from the right side of the canoe shows the motor bar installed, the angle cut in the motor bar, and the hardwood wing nut used to hold the mount in the canoe.

8. Reinforce the motor bar.

The constant stress that a running motor puts on the motor bar requires that you reinforce the motor bar. Remove the base from the canoe, attach the motor bar over it, and then drill a hole large enough for a ¾" (19mm) dowel through the left end block and the motor bar. Expoxy glue the dowel in place, wipe off the excess epoxy, and let the epoxy cure thoroughly. Then trim the dowel flush with the inside of the end block.

9. Apply several coats of exterior polyurethane to the entire mount.

Between coats, let the polyurethane dry completely. Sand it lightly and remove the sanding dust before applying the next coat so it will stick.

Reinforce the motor bar.

Completed, the motor mount can be installed and removed in less than 30 seconds but clamps firmly to the gunwales and withstands the stress of a 4- to 6-horsepower engine running at full throttle.

Starting a Fire in Wet Weather

The first thing to remember about starting a fire during wet weather, especially extended periods, is that dry wood is available. Most standing dead trees are very dry; the rain soaks only the surface. Take your ax and split out the dry wood inside. It is as simple as that.

The best material to get a hot blaze going to ignite your kindling is birch bark. It will burn even soaking wet. However, if you are camping at established camp sites you will find the bark scarce, as thoughtless campers often cut bark from nearby birch trees, causing permanent damage. I have learned to carry some bark with me for use on those wet days. It takes up almost no room and can be pushed and tucked wherever there is an unused corner—for example, under a canoe seat. Replenish your bark supply during daily travels. Loose bark just hangs from the trees, and whatever you can remove without a cutting tool does absolutely no harm.

Making a Splash Guard

The only real disadvantage of mounting a motor on the side of a canoe is that the operator may get thoroughly soaked—especially if running the motor at high speed. Sooner or later you will want to go fast, so use scraps of fiberglass cloth and a little epoxy resin to make this easy splash guard and stop worrying about unwanted showers. The splash guard is a good way to get a little experience with fiberglassing and end up with something useful.

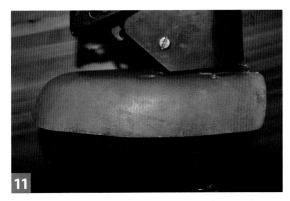

11

Mount the splash guard. This splash guard has been in place many years.

10. Make a splash guard mold and fiberglass it.

Make a mold of wood following the patterns in **Figure 8-2.** The mold does not have to be precision work; you don't even need to enlarge the patterns unless you want to. Just bring the 2" or 2½" (51 or 64mm) block of wood to the approximate shape shown and move on from there. It should be about 10" (254mm) long and 6" (152mm) wide.

When the mold is shaped to your satisfaction, cover it with a clear plastic food wrap to prevent the fiberglass from sticking to the mold. Then simply fiberglass it with about three layers of 6-ounce cloth or the equivalent. Be sure to thoroughly soak the fiberglass cloth with epoxy and then let it cure. Just let the cloth hang down over the sides of the form and leave the back of the form (the squared-off end) free of fiberglass.

When the fiberglass has cured, remove the wood form and cut off the excess fiberglass so you end up with something like that shown in photo 11.

11. Shape and mount the splash guard.

Use a scrap piece of cardboard to make a template of the motor shaft at the point where you want to attach your splash guard. Trace the outline on your fiberglass guard and make the cutout.

Pop-rivet or bolt four strips of sheet metal about ½" (13mm) wide and 4" (102mm) long to the guard, then bend them at a 90° angle and use a stainless steel pipe clamp to secure them to your motor. This attachment method does not requiring modifying your motor or drilling into it, yet the motor guard is secure and permanent.

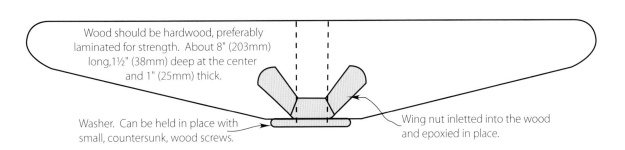

Wood should be hardwood, preferably laminated for strength. About 8" (203mm) long,1½" (38mm) deep at the center and 1" (25mm) thick.

Washer. Can be held in place with small, countersunk, wood screws.

Wing nut inletted into the wood and epoxied in place.

Figure 8-1: Wooden wing nut.

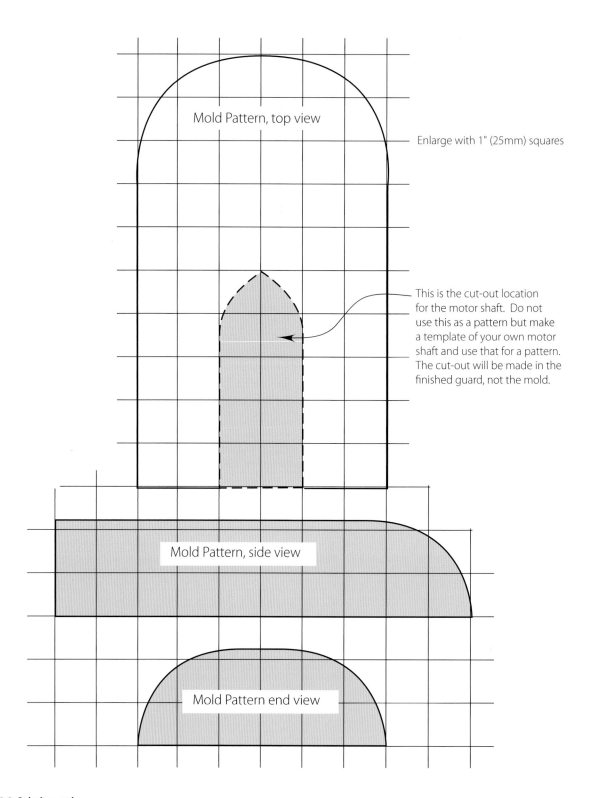

Mold Pattern, top view

Enlarge with 1" (25mm) squares

This is the cut-out location for the motor shaft. Do not use this as a pattern but make a template of your own motor shaft and use that for a pattern. The cut-out will be made in the finished guard, not the mold.

Mold Pattern, side view

Mold Pattern end view

Figure 8-2: Splash guard.

Storing Stove Funnels

If you use a gasoline-burning camp stove, you already know the difficulties of getting your fuel from the can to the stove's tank. A small funnel, preferably filtered, is the obvious answer, but then raises the problem of what to do with the funnel when it is not being used? If it isn't handy you will find it hard to resist the temptation to attempt pouring the fuel directly into the small opening in the tank. Spilled gas is the usual result.

To provide clean storage and keep my funnel readily available, I made a small leather bag with a drawstring on top. Leather is not necessary; any heavy material will do. I made the drawstring long enough to tie it on the outside of my stove, where it hangs when the stove is in use. When I fold the stove for storage or transport, I simply place the funnel bag inside and close the cover. The funnel is always attached to the stove, so there is no danger of losing it and it is always handy when needed.

Repairing Tent Zippers

Spending a night camping during bug season without a tent zipper is no picnic. Many modern nylon tents come equipped with nylon zippers manufacturers describe as "self healing," which I take to mean that they will repair themselves if something goes wrong. Be that as it may, they don't always work.

Many times you can repair these aggravating zippers. Just take the pliers and squeeze the zipper slide together on each side near its narrow end (trailing end when closing). It will take a little experimenting to achieve just the right amount of pressure, so take it easy at first. Usually the problem is caused by some foreign object, such as a piece of the flap, being zipped into the zipper and spreading the slide slightly. You are just putting it back where it belongs. However, the cure doesn't work indefinitely. After a while the sprung slide just will not bring the thing together no matter what, and you will need a new zipper. But with a little care this repair will get you through an outing until you return home and can undertake a more permanent repair.

The vigorous strokes of my son-in-law David Cost blur the bucksaw. I have loaned this saw many times to neighboring campers who took to the woods with only a camp ax or, worse, a hatchet. Also notice the trip box doing triple duty as sawhorse, anchor for the tarp ropes, and food-holder.

Chapter 9

BUCKSAW

There is no substitute for a good saw to maintain a dependable campfire. I have watched campers struggle with axes, hatchets, and too-small camping saws, and the effort they expend seems way beyond the benefits they might receive from the fire. The saws available on the market will give various levels of satisfaction. Most are made to sell (cheap) or were designed by someone who never had to depend on a saw for day-in and day-out wood supply for cooking, warming and bug control. Occasionally, I do see a well-designed camp bucksaw in a sporting goods store—generally built in a home workshop by someone trying to earn extra income. Unfortunately, those people soon discover they cannot earn enough to make it worthwhile, and either give up or price themselves out of business. So if you want a good saw, you will probably have to build it yourself. Besides, the best reason for building your own saw—or, really, any equipment—is for your own satisfaction.

I remember the old woodpile behind our house and the big bucksaw my father used to cut wood to stove length. I took some turns on the old bucksaw myself, but before I was big enough to do any serious sawing, the heating system was converted to coal, and then to oil. The days spent on replenishing the woodpile were gone—until the 1970s when oil prices went out of sight. By then the chainsaw was here.

Remembering that old bucksaw behind the house (about a 36" [914mm] blade), I decided a smaller version would be just the thing for camping. I looked around for what was available for hardware, mainly the blade and turnbuckle, and set about making a frame that would accommodate them. That's how my bucksaw came about. I have been carrying a pair of them on my trips ever since. I carry two saws to avoid disappointing anyone chomping at the bit to help cut wood. Working alone with this saw and a splitting ax, a person can put up enough wood in a half hour or so to last through the evening and for the morning breakfast fire.

I call the other saw in this chapter the Pelkey Saw, after Pete Pelkey of Barre, Vermont, who showed me his original design while we both were attending the Maine Canoe Symposium. He gave me permission to use his design here, his only reward being the knowledge that others would use and appreciate his saw. I imagine that a folding pocket-knife (jackknife) was his inspiration, because his saw's blade folds into the two upright pieces. This makes the saw safe to handle and pack away without a carrying case like the one I use to hold my bucksaw. The completed saw has just three parts: the blade with the connected uprights, the stretcher, and the cord that is twisted to tighten the blade for use. The cord does double duty—it also holds the folded parts together when the saw is stored. The fourth part necessary to assemble the saw for use is a twist stick; Pete reasoned that places where a saw is required will certainly have sticks for that purpose.

People unaccustomed to a saw with a flexible blade often have difficulty keeping the Pelkey saw running straight through a cut; the blade wanders, and the resulting curved cut is much longer than necessary and requires more muscle. This is often caused by too much down pressure on the saw, which causes the blade to twist, especially when the blade is first entering the cut. To prevent this, keep the saw vertical and use only the weight of the saw, especially when the blade is first entering the wood.

Check out both saws and make the one that you think meets your needs.

Getting Ready

It is a good idea to gather all of the materials before starting. If you can't obtain everything as listed, you may need to adjust or alter the original design—and it's better to do that before you start than midway through.

Nearly any good strong hardwood is suitable for making saws. I used oak for these because I had a lot of short pieces of oak left over from other projects. I have also used birch, maple, ash, and cherry with good results. Discarded furniture can be a good source of hardwood for projects like this one, as long as it is made of solid hardwood and not veneer.

Some folks also salvage discarded pallets as a source for hardwood.

Both saws shown in this chapter are designed for a 24" (610mm) blade, which is widely available at hardware stores and farm/home supply centers. However, some dealers don't carry the 24" (610mm) blade, favoring instead 20" or 21" (508 or 533mm). Check your hardware store to see what is available, or look up a place that has the blade you want. A reliable supply is important so you can replace old blades occasionally. The store should also have the rest of the hardware required for whichever saw you make.

Making A Camp Axe (Almost) Foolproof

Whether you go camping to fish, hunt, canoe, or whatever, the people in your group will probably vary as much in their ability to use camp tools as they do in personality. Therefore, many leaders become extremely possessive of their ax, allowing no one to handle it. This might be a good solution for some, but the drawbacks are that only the leader will be able to split wood and novices will not have the opportunity to learn to use an ax properly.

Early on, I decided that I wanted all the help that people wanted to give me—and that included splitting firewood. The most common destroyer of camp axes is the chopper missing the target and hitting the wood with the handle just above the head of the ax. Sooner or later, this will cause the handle to break at this point.

I discovered a solution by accident, while searching for a method of repairing a split ax handle. I took some nylon line (chalk line available from any hardware store) and wrapped it tightly around the handle, from the ax head up about a third of the handle's length. Next I soaked the nylon line with epoxy to make it more durable and withstand the abrasion of constant use. If you don't have epoxy, you could use a good polyurethane varnish to soak the nylon.

Materials

- Bucksaw blade
- Turnbuckle
- 18" to 20" (457 to 508mm) of ³⁄₁₆" or ¼" (5 or 6mm) steel rod OR heavy steel wire
- 5 linear feet of ¾" x 1 ½" (19 x 38mm) hardwood
- (2) 12d common nails
- Sandpaper, 50 and 80 grit
- 1 piece of leather or canvas, 11" x 32" (279 x 812mm)
- Nylon mason's line

Tools

- Table saw**
- Drill press (optional)
- Electric hand drill
- ³⁄₁₆" (5mm) drill bit (may need slightly larger or smaller; see text)
- Butane torch
- ¼" (6mm) wood chisel
- Back saw or fine-tooth saw
- Hammer
- Pencil
- ⁵⁄₁₆" (8mm) straight router bit (optional)
- ½" (13mm) round-over router bit (optional)
- Router (optional)
- Narrow kerf circular saw blade
- Means to measure angle (sliding bevel, protractor)
- 4-in-1 rasp
- Sander (optional)

** Necessary, but limited use— borrow or beg if you don't have one

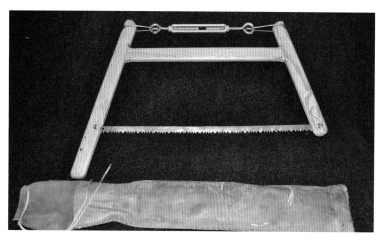

This bucksaw has accompanied me on countless canoe trips. I cannot estimate the amount of firewood it has cut down and bucked up over the years. The storage bag is a necessity to keep the parts together and to prevent injury from the sharp blade.

Making a Bucksaw

1. Cut the wooden parts.

Rip up enough ¾" x 1½" (19 x 38mm) hardwood to make the three wooden parts of the saw, then cut to exact lengths using the dimensions given in **Figure 9-1**. For blades that are not 24" (610mm), simply add or subtract the difference between your blade and the 24" (610mm) blade shown.

2. Locate and mark all holes, slots, and mortises.

Use **Figure 9-1**. The mortises in the two upright pieces should be ⁵⁄₁₆" (8mm) wide, 1 ½" (38mm) long, and ¾" (19mm) deep. Most mortises in this book are ½"

(13mm) deep, but the extra depth helps these mortises function without glue and stabilizes the uprights when you apply pressure with the turnbuckle.

3. Mark and drill holes for the pins.

Before drilling the holes in the frame, decide what you will use as pins to secure the blade to the wooden parts: the pin size dictates the hole size. These were made from 12d nails with the head hacksawed off and the end heated red-hot with a butane torch and then bent into a loop so the pin can be tied to the wooden frame. The fit should be snug but not binding. The size of the hole for the pin tie (upper hole) is not critical; usually the same size will do.

4. Cut the mortises.

A drill press and ⁵⁄₁₆" (8mm) straight router bit make cutting the mortises easy. See photo 4, page 41. If you don't have those, a little time with a ¼" (6mm) wood chisel and a hammer will make short work of the cutting job.

5. Cut the slots for the blade.

The last operation on the two uprights, cutting the slots for the blade, is tricky and can be dangerous; I use a table saw with as thin a blade as possible. I have tried to come up with another practical method for cutting these slots, but nothing so far. A specialty handsaw with teeth on a curved edge would probably work, but I've never had one available. Be careful.

Adjust the saw fence so the cut will be exactly in the middle of the stock. It is a good idea to use scrap material the same thickness as your stock to make sure the slot will be centered. The safest way to make this cut is to clamp the stock to the saw's rip fence with the saw blade down. Then, with the saw running, raise the saw to the desired height. **Figure 9-1** shows the saw kerf in relation to the pin holes.

6. Cut the stretcher tenons and fit them into the mortises.

The ends of the stretcher are cut at 77° or 13°, depending on how you read it. When you have the ends cut to proper length and at the correct angle, measure back ¾" (19mm) and mark for the tenon shoulder. Mark all four sides so you can see it however you turn the piece. The tenons should be ⁵⁄₁₆" (8mm) thick and across the entire width of the stretcher (1 ½"—38mm). Note in **Figure 9-1** that the long end of the tenon is angled so it enters the mortise (cut at 90°) without binding. Determine the exact amount to remove as you fit the tenon into the mortise.

Do careful handwork on your mortises and tenons to get a good snug fit that does not bind. Remember, this saw is made to be taken down for packing, so you want to be able to assemble and disassemble it without the parts binding up on you. On the other hand, the strength and longevity of this tool depend on a good fit of parts that will go together and come apart many, many of times.

Finishing a Bucksaw

7. Fashion loops to use with the turnbuckle.

With the wooden parts made and a blade and turnbuckle in hand, you need some sort of loop to go over the top of the uprights. The loops shown below right are made of ³⁄₁₆" (5mm) rod with the ends brazed together. Welding tools are the best way to do this, so getting someone who has them to help you is probably the best solution. If you can't do that, just heat and bend the ends of your rods into small loops and interlock them (like a chain). First make sure the loop is through the hole in the turnbuckle and large enough to hook up and tighten. There are other possible ways to hook up the turnbuckle, including making multiple wraps with a small wire. You may have a better idea. Whatever you do, make sure the loop is strong; tightening that turnbuckle applies a lot of pressure to it.

8. Assemble the saw, shape, and sand.

Put the saw together. If everything fits okay, go ahead and finish up the wooden parts. Shape the top ends of the uprights as shown in Figure 9-1, or design your own; they just need a shallow notch to hold the turnbuckle loop. You can round over the other ends of the uprights, or shape them to suit your fancy. Round off all the corners of your stock so the saw frame feels nice in your hands. A router

with a ½" (13mm) radius round-over bit does that nicely, or you can easily do it with a rasp. Then sand the parts until you are happy with them. This usually requires, at minimum, 50-grit paper followed by 80-grit. I usually don't go finer than that. This is, after all, a tool to use in the woods—but if you want to sand to 120-grit, go for it!

9. Finish the wood.

Write your name, address, and date on the wood, then finish it according to your preference. You could use exterior polyurethane, linseed oil, or nothing at all. You're finished! The next time you pull into camp after a long, cold day you will appreciate having a good, high-quality saw to help get the fire going.

Making a Bucksaw Case

You will want something to put the pieces in when you are packed and traveling. The case below was made of a piece of 11" x 32" (279 x 812mm) leather folded in half and laced with nylon mason's line, which is available from most hardware stores. The 11" (279mm) width should be okay for any saw, but make sure your case will hold the longest part of your saw, which should be the blade. Allow an additional 6" or 8" (152 or 203mm) for a flap at the top; attaching some ties makes it a secure closure that will keep the parts from falling out. The rivets at the bottom of the case hold a piece of leather on the inside to keep the blade from cutting the lacing; this extra precaution is not necessary for light to moderate use. Other materials will make a suitable saw case, including canvas or even an old pair of jeans.

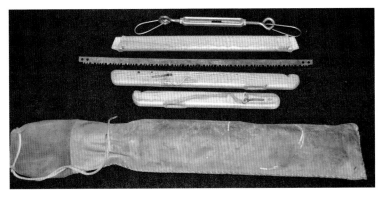

The bucksaw is easy to break down and reassemble. Here the parts are ready to be placed in the storage bag. Humidity made the steel blades rust, but this does no harm and will wear off with the first couple of cuts.

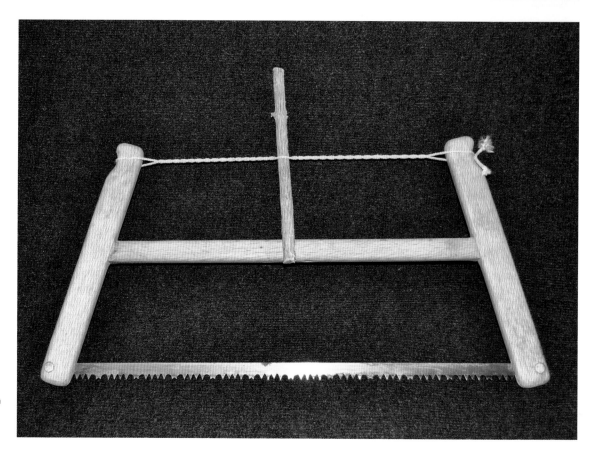

Open for use, this Pelkey saw looks very much like my bucksaw except for the tightening mechanism, which consists of a rope twisted with a stick.

Making a Pelkey Saw

Materials

- Bucksaw blade
- Sandpaper, 50 and 80 grit
- 2 pieces of ¾" x 1 ½" (19 x 38mm) hardwood for uprights (length depends on saw blade; see Figure 9-2)
- 1 piece of ¾" x 1" (19 x 25mm) hardwood for stretcher (length depends on saw blade; see Figure 9-2)
- 1 piece of parachute cord or ⅛" (3mm) braided nylon cord about 3' (915mm) long
- 2 machine bolts, ¼" x ¾" (6 x 19mm)
- 2 lock nuts, ¼" (6mm)
- 2 flat washers, ¼" (6mm) (optional)

Tools

- Table saw**
- Drill press (optional)
- Electric hand drill
- Drill bit, ½" (13mm) for counterbore
- Drill bit, ¼" (6mm)
- Pencil
- Round-over router bit, ¼" (6mm) (optional)
- Router (optional)
- Means to measure angle (sliding bevel, protractor)
- 4-in-1 rasp
- Sander (optional)

  ** Necessary, but limited use—borrow or beg if you don't have one

1. Cut out the stretcher and the two uprights.
Start with the dimensions listed for the length of your blade in **Figure 9-2**. Then drill the blade attachment hole:

Start by cutting out the three wooden parts shown in **Figure 9-2**, two uprights and one stretcher. Next drill the ¼" (6mm) blade attachment hole; if you do the ½" (13mm) counterbore, it is easier to drill that before you drill the smaller hole.

2. Cut the saw kerfs and try assembling the blade and the uprights.
The saw kerfs should be lengthwise and across the end where you drilled the blade attachment hole. When the kerfs are finished, do a trial assembly of the blade with the uprights; blades from different manufacturers can vary a bit, so you may need to make some adjustments. Make sure the two uprights are not too long as you fold them over the teeth of the blade; if they are, just take a little off the top of each one until they fold neatly into place. The uprights must swivel around in about a 280° arc from their assembled position to the stored position. Also check that the saw kerfs are deep enough to accommodate the blade.

My bucksaw and the Pelkey Saw stored for travel. I always carried two saws on my trips.

3. Make the mortises and tenons.

Use **Figure 9-2** for a pattern. The initial length of the stretcher extends beyond the finished tenon to make the initial cuts for the ¼" (6mm) tenons easier. If you use the mortise-and-tenon method, cut the mortises in the uprights before you cut the tenons in the stretcher.

If you prefer not to make tenons, you can drill and glue a dowel in each side instead, then drill corresponding holes (instead of the mortise) in the uprights to accommodate the dowels. That hole should be a little oversize for ease in assembly. If you decide on the dowel method, use the shorter stretcher length shown in **Figure 9-2**.

4. Finish shaping and sanding the saw.

Make two elongated holes near the center of the stretcher. When you disassemble the saw for storage, you will put the cord through those holes and then wrap it around the folded blade and uprights at the shallow dip. Rounding off the sharp edges makes the saw more comfortable to use. I used a small rounding cutter in a router, but if you don't have one, a rasp would work. Sand the wooden parts one last time.

5. Assemble and finish the saw.

The saw slot holding the ends of the blade is a lot wider than the thickness of the blade, which allows it to twist on the bolt that is holding it. To prevent this, I put a ¼" (6mm) flat washers in each saw kerf along with the blade during final assembly. The machine bolt goes through both the washer and the blade. It takes a little time and fiddling around to get the alignment of the blade, washer, and hole in the upright, but this is a one-time thing during final assembly and it makes the saw better. You can finish your saw with exterior polyurethane, linseed oil, or nothing at all. Enjoy your Pelkey saw, and think of Pete when you use it!

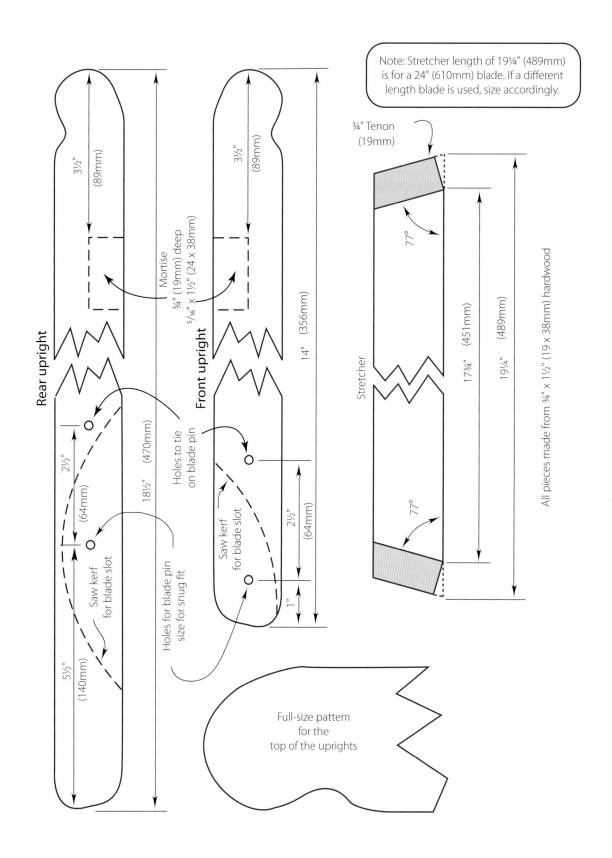

Note: Stretcher length of 19¼" (489mm) is for a 24" (610mm) blade. If a different length blade is used, size accordingly.

¾" Tenon (19mm)

Rear upright

Front upright

Mortise ¾" (19mm) deep ⁵/₁₆" x 1½" (24 x 38mm)

3½" (89mm)

3½" (89mm)

14" (356mm)

Holes to tie on blade pin

Saw kerf for blade slot

2½" (64mm)

18½" (470mm)

Holes for blade pin size for snug fit

Saw kerf for blade slot

2½" (64mm)

1"

5½" (140mm)

Stretcher

77°

77°

17¾" (451mm)

19¼" (489mm)

All pieces made from ¾" x 1½" (19 x 38mm) hardwood

Full-size pattern for the top of the uprights

Figure 9-1: Wood parts of bucksaw.

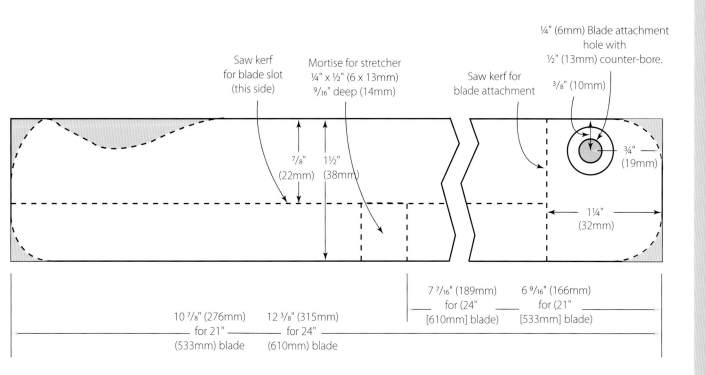

¼" (6mm) Blade attachment hole with ½" (13mm) counter-bore.

Saw kerf for blade slot (this side)

Mortise for stretcher ¼" x ½" (6 x 13mm) ⁹/₁₆" deep (14mm)

Saw kerf for blade attachment

³/₈" (10mm)

⁷/₈" (22mm)

1½" (38mm)

¾" (19mm)

1¼" (32mm)

7 ⁷/₁₆" (189mm) for (24" [610mm] blade)

6 ⁹/₁₆" (166mm) for (21" [533mm] blade)

10 ⁷/₈" (276mm) for 21" (533mm) blade

12 ³/₈" (315mm) for 24" (610mm) blade

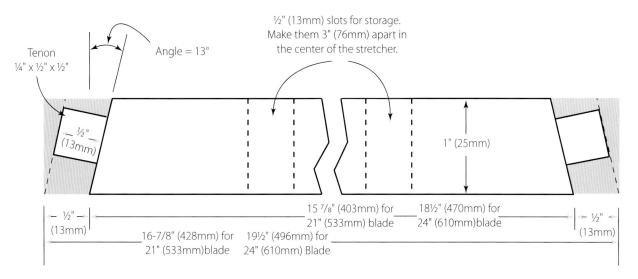

Tenon ¼" x ½" x ½"

Angle = 13°

½" (13mm) slots for storage. Make them 3" (76mm) apart in the center of the stretcher.

½" (13mm)

1" (25mm)

½" (13mm)

½" (13mm)

15 ⁷/₈" (403mm) for 21" (533mm) blade

18½" (470mm) for 24" (610mm)blade

16-7/8" (428mm) for 21" (533mm)blade

19½" (496mm) for 24" (610mm) Blade

Figure 9-2: Wood parts of Pelkey saw.

Chapter 10

HATBAND

My hatband, made of ⅛" (3mm) walnut and what I think of as "modeled silhouettes." Experienced carvers probably have another name for them. I glued on the cutouts and gave them a little shape with small carving chisels. The spacers are pieces cut from a small antler and then drilled.

Materials	Tools
■ Wood of choice 1 ½" x ¾" x 18" (38 x 19 x 457mm)	■ Band saw
■ Nylon mason's line	■ Rule
■ Spacer buttons (optional—you could just tie a knot)	■ Pencil
■ Sandpaper, various grits	■ Square
■ Exterior polyurethane	■ Drill with ⅛" (3mm) drill bit
	■ Sandpaper

I think it is great when you can wear something that tells a little about yourself—who you are, what you do, what your interests are, and that you are proud of it all. A personal hatband does that for the outdoorsman and does it quietly, but with class. There is no end to the designs you can use. Some suggestions are shown, but you can be creative and make your own or shamelessly copy from somewhere else. This is a fun project to work on at odd times when not much else is happening.

You can be as creative as your skills allow you to be in decorating the band. The hats above and on page 108 show panels with cutout silhouettes glued in place and then modeled with small carving chisels. If you are skilled at carving you can create a real masterpiece by doing relief carvings of your favorite subjects. If your skills lean toward painting

you can use that medium. Some have used a scroll saw to make their designs. Woodburning, also known as pyrography, is a good way to do the decoration and it is easy to do. But you know what you can do. Make it fun and make it *you*!

The wood can be just about anything you have on hand. If you are going to woodburn the images, a light-colored wood such as pine, cedar, birch, or maple would be good. If you choose to do carvings, use your favorite carving wood. Strength is not a factor here so hard or soft wood will work equally well.

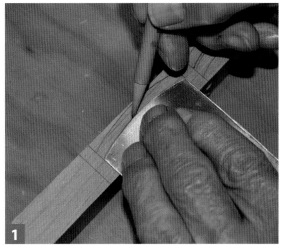

Trace the panels. It is a good idea to make a solid pattern from Figure 10-1 so you can trace out the panels. I used aluminum flashing, but heavy cardboard or thin plywood would work. The wood shown is 1½" (38mm) wide, marked in 2⅜" (60mm) segments; each segment yields two panels. Make sure there's enough left over to give you something to safely hang on to when cutting out the last ones.

Cut the panels. A band saw is the best tool for cutting the panels. The small space between segments allows for over-cutting. Note the four pre-drilled holes.

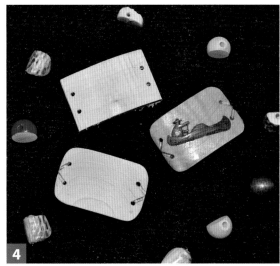

Assemble the band. Panels in three stages of completion, surrounded by spacer buttons. The optional grooves shown in the two finished panels allow the nylon lace to lay a little neater. You can cut them with a Dremel tool or a sharp chisel or knife.

1. Make a panel template and transfer it onto the wood.

The finished wood panels will be 1½" (38mm) by 2⅜" (86mm) and ⅛" to ¼" (3 to 6mm) thick; I prefer about 3⁄16" (5mm). You can vary the size to suit yourself, but these work out well. They also have a slight curve, which you can trace from **Figure 10-1**. You can cut the panels from a block of wood that is cut to the size given above, but it is easier to cut the curved pieces out of a longer piece that is cut to width, (1½" [38mm] wide). That way you can cut as many curved pieces as possible from each segment and then cut them to length. This makes them a little easier and safer to handle.

You will need seven to nine panels; I have a large head and I use eight.

2. Carefully cut, drill, and sand the panels.

Use a ⅛" (3mm) drill bit and make the holes ½" (13mm) apart. You can drill the holes before cutting the panels from the block, if you wish.

3. Decorate the panels.

Choose or create a design and trace it onto the panel with carbon paper or transfer it with a hot iron. All transferring requires is that you make a copy with a copy machine, place the image on the wood, and press down with a hot flat iron. The image will transfer beautifully. Try it on a piece of scrap wood to see if you want to use this method. The image will be reversed, but that is usually no problem unless it includes writing. In that case you will need to hand-trace or reverse the image by some means before placing it on the wood. If you plan to scroll saw the design onto the panel, you can glue on a paper pattern.

4. Assemble the band.

The spacer buttons I used are pieces of deer antler. This is a nice way to use the antlers of a small buck that isn't large enough to rate a wall mounting, but still has meaning, and a memory, for you. The lacing material is nylon mason's line, available from most hardware stores. Wooden beads are available at most craft stores in colors or plain wood; just flatten one side. You can also eliminate the spacers and simply tie a knot between the panels.

5. Finish the band.

When I had my band completely decorated and assembled, I dipped the whole thing in a can of exterior polyurethane and hung it up to dry. This seemed to give it just the right degree of stiffness to hold together the way a band should. Try to keep the ends of the nylon dry during the dipping. This will make it easier to tie it in the back when finished. To attach the band, just tack it to the hat in three or four places with a needle and thread to keep it secure and complete the project.

Good luck with your hatband. I would enjoy hearing and seeing what you come up with, so get the creative juices flowing and go to work!

Dot's hatband, cut from ⅛" (3mm) cherry, with spacers carved from the same cherry used for the cutouts. Hers is a little newer than mine because her previous hat and band were blown off as we struggled to get our group ashore after being caught in a sudden squall.

Figure 10-1: Panel pattern.

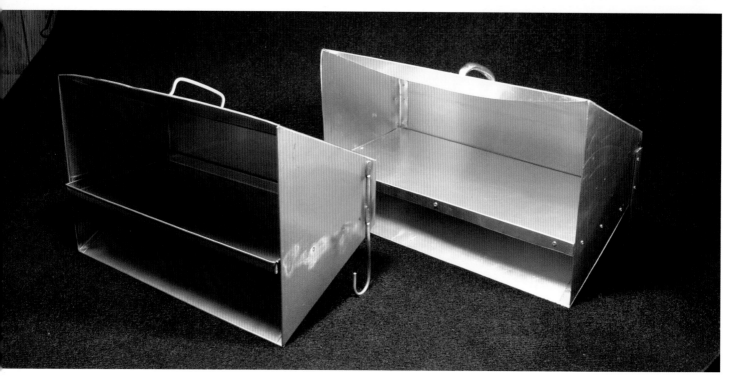

A professionally made oven (left) and the one I made to demonstrate for this chapter (right). The main difference is the cooking shelf. Mine is not removable, so it requires a separate baking pan. In the pro model, the shelf and the pan are one.

Chapter 11

REFLECTOR OVEN

Many guests on my guided canoe trips hired me so they could learn enough to eventually guide future family outings. One thing that really impressed them was baking with a reflector oven; they almost always asked where they could buy one. At the time I only had one source, and considered that oven far from satisfactory. I decided that instructions on how to build an oven would help alleviate this problem. You will find three sources of first-rate ovens in this book. The first source is you: make your own. The other two are Maine outdoorsmen who will be happy to fill your needs with ovens they use themselves.

A few years ago, I discussed reflector ovens with David Lewis at the Maine Canoe Symposium. I told him I thought "reflector" was a poor name for the ovens because, after more than thirty years of daily baking on my canoe trips, I didn't think reflection had much do with it. David started nodding his head, and the longer I talked the faster his head nodded. As it turned out, his research on reflector ovens and my years afield with them had brought us both to the same conclusion. The trapping of hot air around the food is far more important than any benefit from shiny reflector surfaces. In fact, David has gone so far as to state that darkened (not sooty) surfaces cause the oven to bake better than do shiny surfaces. I can neither confirm nor deny his theory.

David's research into various ovens convinced him that the old-timers had it right. He analyzed and tested numerous examples of antique non-collapsible ovens to determine the proper proportions and angles. The plans and instructions in this chapter incorporate the essential components that made those old ovens work so well. **Figure 11-1** is synopsis of his research.

Materials
- Sheet aluminum .032" (0.8128 mm)—size to make selected oven
- Pop rivets, ⅛" (3mm), ¼" (6mm) reach
- ¹⁄₁₆" x ¾" (4 x 19mm) aluminum angle (optional)
- ¹⁄₁₆" x 1" (4 x 25mm) aluminum angle (optional)
- Door handle (optional)

Tools
- Drill
- ⅛" (3mm) drill bit
- Pencil
- Pop-rivet gun
- Metal-cutting shears
- File
- Rule or measuring tape
- Hacksaw
- Framing square

Learning from History

I once took a group on a month-long canoe trip encompassing three of Maine's northern rivers. I used my oven every day, and every day the metal surfaces turned darker and darker. I remember thinking each day that I should clean the metal, but I kept putting off the job. In spite of the darkening, however, the oven didn't seem to lose any of its effectiveness. That's when I started thinking about how the ovens work and about how "reflector" was perhaps a misnomer. "Baker" would be a better name for them. In fact, "baker" is what the old-timers called them.

The bakers have a long history in my state. Maine is still more than 92 percent forested, so wood harvesting was and is an important industry. Until about 1970, river driving was the principal means of moving wood. In the early years, the cooks for these drives prepared food over open fires and in huge bakers on both sides of the cooking fires. The following is an excerpt from the chapter "Jill-Pokes in the Willywags," an account of an early river drive on the Allagash River, in my book Allagash. The description of the cooking setup closely resembles that of David Lewis' at left.

The cookees [cook's helpers] set up the cook's tent, then built a fireplace with two rows of stones that served as andirons and a bar supported by two crotched sticks driven into the ground, on which the kettles were hung on iron hooks. The cook began to roll out sourdough biscuits and gingerbread on his large breadboard on top of a flour barrel. These [would be] baked in big reflector bakers on each side of the open fire. The cookees cut wood, dug a hole, and filled it with wood. Later they would place the big kettle of beans in the hole so the beans could bake overnight.

I cannot imagine those busy cookees having the time each day to polish the reflecting surfaces of their bakers, and in researching old-time river drives I never came across any mention of it. It seems to me that such an onerous chore would certainly have warranted a mention in the literature.

Once you accept the premise that bakers cook principally by trapping hot air, not reflection, the shapes of the old-time ovens (and David's designs) make a lot of sense. Take a look at **Figure 11-1.** It is immediately apparent that the angle of the antique oven will trap more hot air, and hold it better, than the modern collapsible oven. I have cooked successfully for many years with a collapsible oven. But the first time I saw Dave's comparison, one note jumped out at me: "need an inferno to cook." I readily agreed with that note, because I certainly did burn a lot of wood to get the job done.

David Lewis demonstrates outdoor cooking at the Maine Canoe Symposium. Note the bread baking in the oven while other parts of the meal hang over the small cooking fire.

Things to Consider

I am not a metal worker, so the methods I use to make the baker are just common-sense ways to get the job done with a minimum of tools. In fact, the only metal-working tools needed are metal-cutting shears, a drill, and a pop-rivet gun. In short, if I can do it, anyone can.

David believes a stainless steel baker does a better job than one made of aluminum. I think this may be a very fine distinction, because I know that aluminum works just fine. I also know that for the amateur metal worker (like me), aluminum is a lot easier to work with than steel. Therefore, I recommend that you use aluminum if you plan to make it yourself. If you want stainless steel, take the plans to a pro or purchase one from one of the suppliers listed in "Resources and Supplies."

David's stainless ovens have a removable shelf that serves as a baking pan. However, when I looked at my hands and saw how black they were from handling the aluminum, I didn't want to cook directly on the aluminum surface. So the oven I made has a permanent shelf and requires a separate baking pan.

Choose the size you need. The large oven will take care of eight to twelve people. Use the medium size if you cook for four to six people. A small family or group consisting of two to four people can get by with the small oven. Unless space is a large consideration, however, I recommend choosing a larger size than you think you need. You can double up and, for example, bake your bread or biscuits at the same time as a pan of brownies or some cookies.

To illustrate this chapter, I built the large oven from David's plans. I chose .032" (0.8128mm)-sheet aluminum, and the weight seems to be about right. I made one a few years ago using a lighter material, and the baker seemed a little flimsy. By doing the layout described in step 1, I saw that I needed a piece 32" x 36" (812 x 915mm). There was plenty left over for the smaller pieces like legs and the handle. However, I decided to buy some aluminum angles for the legs and the shelf support. This material is available in ¹⁄₁₆" x ¾" (2 x 19mm) and ¹⁄₁₆" by 1" (2 x 25mm) from many hardware stores. I bought a piece of each, using the 1" (25mm) for the legs and the ¾" (19mm) for the shelf supports. The ¾" (19mm) would have worked well for both. I also bought an inexpensive door handle for the oven's handle.

Making an Oven

1. Plan your cuts.

Use paper patterns only to determine how to lay out your parts with the least waste. Do your actual layout directly on the metal itself, using the information in **Figure 11-3** as a guide. Use a solid straightedge and a framing square, making sure all sides are square and the dimensions are accurate. Follow the old craftsman's adage, "Measure twice, cut once." The opposite seldom works out well. Lay out and cut the four larger pieces first, then lay out the smaller ones.

2. Cut and smooth the parts.

Use a good pair of metal-cutting shears to cut the four large aluminum parts to size. Work carefully and make accurate cuts exactly on your lines. It is easier to cut out two appropriately sized rectangles for the sides and then cut to final shape. This uses slightly more material, but saves you the irritation of making complicated cuts in the large sheet of material. When the major parts are cut, lay out and cut out the smaller parts. Then use a file to smooth and round off all sharp edges so you don't get cut making the oven or using it.

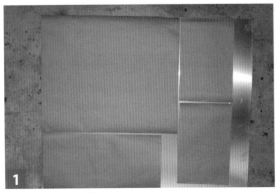

Determine the best layout.

3. Measure, mark, and score the fold lines.

When all pieces are safe to handle, carefully measure and mark the fold lines on all parts. When you are satisfied that all lines are accurately placed and square, you are ready to make the folds or bends. I used the sharp corner of a wood chisel to score the lines; just a couple of light passes creates a crease in the metal, which will help create sharp, neat bends. Notice that in the photo the straightedge is clamped down firmly over the metal part. I recommend this because you want to keep side pressure on the straightedge to ensure that line goes straight. If it isn't clamped down, it is likely to slip, especially on the longer pieces. You want only one score for each bend.

4. Bend the parts.

If you have access to sheet-metal bending tools, you can ignore my instructions on bending. Otherwise, look how I handled the long bends of the large pieces. I used the edge of my table saw, but any sharp edge you can find will work as well. If you have nothing suitable around the house or shop, get a piece of angle iron or aluminum or even a hardwood board and clamp it to the edge of a table or bench for a nice sharp edge. Place the scored line directly over the sharp edge and clamp a board on top to hold the metal part firmly in place. Using your hands, press down slowly, with the pressure spread out as much as possible. The metal will make a nice sharp bend right on your scored line.

To make bends on some of the shorter pieces, especially the ¾" (19mm) tabs, I just clamped them as described above, with the tab projecting over the edge. Then I took a hardwood block, to spread the pressure, and tapped the tab down with a hammer.

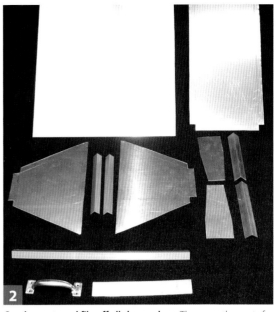

Cut the parts and file off all sharp edges. These are the parts for a large oven. Two versions of a handle are in the lower left, with two versions of the oven's legs in the lower right.

Score the fold lines.

Bend the parts. For sharp bends, clamp the part firmly on a hard object with a sharp edge (preferably metal—here we used the side of my table saw).

5. Trim edges.

When all the tabs are bent, you will notice that the ends of some must be trimmed before the oven is assembled. The fit of the two sides into the 4" (102mm) back panel is critical; I suggest making the back of each side perhaps ⅟₁₆" (2mm) or so less than the 4" (102mm) on the plans. If the sides turns out a little too small, it is easier to bend the tabs out a little to fill the space than it is to make them fit if the sides are too large. The long front shelf support is missing from the photo.

Because I opted to use the heavier aluminum angle for shelf supports, I removed the end tabs of the shelf. The front of the shelf is the closest part of the oven to the heat source, and on previous ovens I found that the weight of the food and the extreme heat combined to make the shelf bend down in the middle. To prevent that, I bent the front tab at a 90° angle so the long ⅟₁₆" (2mm) aluminum angle could fit inside.

I bent the rear tab of the shelf at an angle resembling that shown in **Figure 7-2**. This allows me to rivet the back tab to the bottom panel, strengthening the shelf even more. Bending the back tab all the way, so there is a double thickness at the edge (a hem), would probably work as well. You can leave the front right angle bend as is, but repeated heating may cause it to warp and sag, so I recommend riveting on a piece of angle aluminum to prevent that.

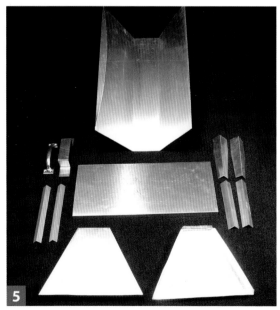

These are bent and ready for assembly. The bending includes the ¾" (19mm) tabs on the ends at the bottom of the photo, although it is difficult to see here. Note the two handle versions on the left and the two leg versions on the right.

Assembling an Oven

6. Clamp and then rivet the sides, top, and bottom together.

Use clamps to hold the side's tabs to the top and bottom panels. Make any adjustments needed. Drill and pop-rivet the back panel first. This will ensure that it is pulled firmly in place. Proceed with riveting the top and bottom panels to the side's tabs. Repeat with the other side.

7. Install the permanent shelf.

Doing this properly requires some care. First make sure your shelf supports will fit at the proper level. This requires cutting the back of the support at an angle, so the top of it meets the back of the oven exactly at the bend between the back and bottom panels. Once the angle is cut, clamp the two supports in place. Make sure the shelf fits in place properly. In the large oven, it should be 4" (102mm) above the bottom of the bottom panel in front, and the rear of the shelf should meet the bend between the back and bottom panels.

When you are satisfied with the fit, clamp the shelf to the supports. Then remove the shelf and supports (still clamped together), and rivet them together. Re-install the shelf and supports and rivet them to the sides. This clamping procedure is necessary because a drill will not fit inside the oven to drill for rivets. If you have a right-angle drill, you can avoid the clamping and removal. Of course, if you opt to make a removable shelf, just rivet the shelf supports in place on each side of the oven.

8. Attach the remaining pieces.

Now the hard part is done. All that remains is to attach the optional front shelf support, the legs, and the handle. You can see the rivets used to hold the long shelf support to the front of the shelf on photo 8. Attach the legs so the rear of the shelf (which should be at the bend between the back and bottom panels) is 4" (102mm) above the ground (for the large oven). This ensures that your shelf is level. Rivet on the handle and you are done!

Traveling with an Oven

The main thing that folding, or collapsible, ovens have going for them is that they take up very little space in your box, pack, or whatever you use to haul your kitchen gear. The oven you build from the plans here might look bulky, but it actually packs very compactly.

David's gear box (wannigan) allows him to put the oven in it open side up, then fill it with his silverware roll and other small kitchen items. It is also possible to pack other items around the smaller end of the oven (on the bottom of the box), so the oven itself takes up very little space in the box.

People have their own ways of doing things, and mine are a little different from David's. My kitchen box is low and long so it can be backpacked when necessary (page 87), and the oven does not fit in it. So I make the oven itself a box, constructing a cover for it and filling it with kitchen items just as David does. The cover is similar to the ones on the food boxes in "Trip Box," and its sides need to extend down only ¾" (19mm).

I fiberglass the outside of the cover finish the inside with epoxy so I can use it for food preparation while in camp. Please note that Gougeon Brothers, manufacturer of West System epoxy, does not promote or recommend the product for use on food contact surfaces. However, they state that they are not aware of any health consequences associated with the use of West System products in those applications. Make up your own mind.
The oven itself is not waterproof, but with the shoebox-style cover it sheds rain—and besides, nothing I carry in it will be ruined if it gets wet. I secure the cover with a heavy-duty bungee cord. You could equip the oven and cover with latches of some kind to lock them together, but I am an advocate of the KISS principle (Keep It Simple, Stupid), so I use the bungee cord.

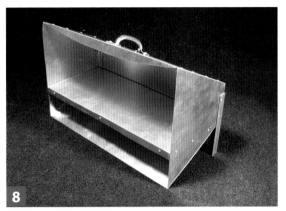

8

Attach the remaining pieces. I opted for the door handle and the angle legs.

A cover turns my non-collapsible oven into a box.

Comparing the Old and the New

By David Lewis

Antiques

Based on my measurements of several old ovens, there seems to be a "mystical" relationship of the parts:

- The angle between the panels is approximately 50°.
- The angles between the top and bottom panels to the shelf height are approximately equal.
- The shelf height is located lower than the hypothetical intersection of the panels.
- The height of the back panel is approximately equal to its height above the ground.

I have incorporated these "rules" into the designs shown here.

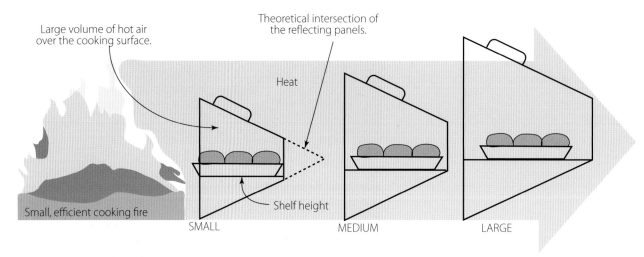

Modern collapsible

In the newer ovens, the relationship between the parts are different:

- The angle between the panels is 90°.
- The angles between the top and bottom panels to the shelf height are equal.
- The shelf height is located exactly at the intersection of the panels.

These observations are based on measurements of two commercially-available ovens which shall remain nameless, and information and patterns available on the Internet.

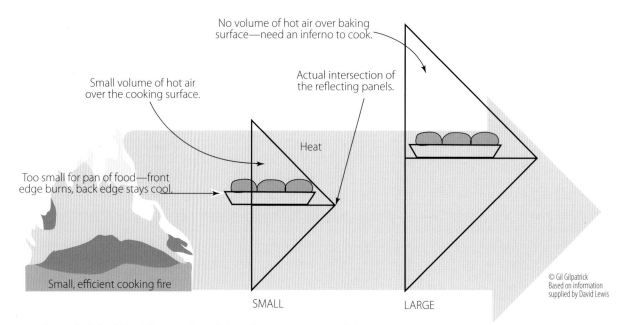

Figure 11-1: David Lewis's comparison of old and new reflector oven designs.

Shelf (end view)

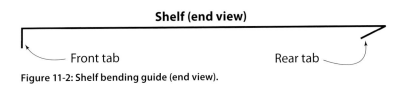

Front tab   Rear tab

Figure 11-2: Shelf bending guide (end view).

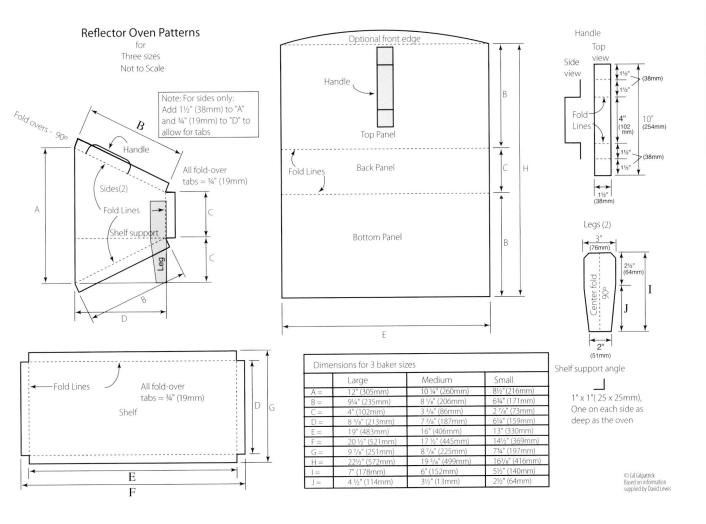

Reflector Oven Patterns
for
Three sizes
Not to Scale

Note: For sides only:
Add 1½" (38mm) to "A"
and ¾" (19mm) to "D" to
allow for tabs

Fold overs - 90°

B

Handle

Sides(2)

Fold Lines

Shelf support

Leg

All fold-over
tabs = ¾" (19mm)

A

C

C

B

D

Optional front edge

Handle

Top Panel

Fold Lines

Back Panel

Bottom Panel

B

C

H

B

E

Handle

Top
view

Side
view

Fold
Lines

1½" (38mm)
1½"

4"
(102
mm)

10"
(254mm)

1½" (38mm)
1½"

1½"
(38mm)

Legs (2)

3"
(76mm)

2½"
(64mm)

Center fold
90°

I

J

2"
(51mm)

Shelf support angle

1" x 1"(25 x 25mm),
One on each side as
deep as the oven

Fold Lines

All fold-over
tabs = ¾" (19mm)

Shelf

D

G

E

F

Dimensions for 3 baker sizes			
	Large	Medium	Small
A =	12" (305mm)	10 ¼" (260mm)	8½" (216mm)
B =	9¼" (235mm)	8 ⅛" (206mm)	6¾" (171mm)
C =	4" (102mm)	3 ⅜" (86mm)	2 ⅞" (73mm)
D =	8 ⅜" (213mm)	7 ⅜" (187mm)	6¼" (159mm)
E =	19" (483mm)	16" (406mm)	13" (330mm)
F =	20 ½" (521mm)	17 ½" (445mm)	14½" (369mm)
G =	9 ⅞" (251mm)	8 ⅞" (225mm)	7¾" (197mm)
H =	22½" (572mm)	19 ⅝" (499mm)	16⅜" (416mm)
I =	7" (178mm)	6" (152mm)	5½" (140mm)
J =	4 ½" (114mm)	3½" (13mm)	2½" (64mm)

Figure 11-3: Reflector oven plans, three sizes.

RESOURCES AND SUPPLIES

Supplies

Pack Straps, Bags, and Other Camping Gear
The Military Trail Gear Shop
"GI Type Enhanced Shoulder
Straps" (also available through
www.amazon.com)
899 Park Ave.
Huntington, NY 11743
www.themilitarytril.com

Epoxy and Fiberglassing
**Gougeon Brothers, Inc. (Catalog
& catalog on line)**
100 Paterson Ave.
Bay City, MI 48707-0908
(517) 684-6881
www.westsystem.com

Epoxy and Fiberglassing
Raka, Inc. (Catalog on line)
3490 Oleander Ave.,
Ft. Pierce, Florida 34982
PH. 772.489.4070
www.raka.com

Cane for Seats
**The H.H. Perkins Co. (Catalog &
catalog on line)**
10 South Bradley Road
Woodbridge CT 06525
800-462-6660
www.hhperkins.com

Cane for Seats
**Conneticut Cane and Reed
Company**
P.O. Box 762
Manchester, CT 06045
800-227-8498
www.caneandreed.com

Canvas Bag for Pack Frame
Jane Barron
Alder Stream Canvas
21 Salem Road
Kingfield, ME 04947
207-265-5104
jbarronsew@gmail.com
http://alderstream.wcha.org/

Reflector Ovens
David Lewis
183 Rankin Road
Buxton, ME 04093
207-929-4107
fdmsl@sacoriver.net

Reflector Ovens
Pole and Paddle Canoe
Don Merchant
PO Box 68
Limerick, ME 04048
207-929-8931

I am glad to answer questions about your project. When you email me
please use a subject I will identify with this book. Example: "Reflector
Oven". Because my email address is out there on my website for all to
see, I receive hundreds of emails each week. If I don't recognize the
subject or the sender, I delete them without opening.

Resources

Bass Pro Shops (Catalog)
2500 E. Kearney
Springfield, MO 65898-0123
800-227-7776
www.basspro.com

**REI [Recreational Equipment
Inc.] (Catalog)**
Sumner, WA 98352-0001
800-426-4840
www.rei.com

Gander Mountain (Catalog)
111 Red Banks Rd
Greenville, NC 27858
888-5GANDER
www.gandermountain.com

L.L. Bean (Catalog)
Freeport, ME 04033
800-221-4221
www.llbean.com

Cabela's (Catalog)
One Cabella Drive
Sidney, NE 69160
800-237-4444
www.cabelas.com

Country Ways (Catalog)
6001 Lyndale Ave. S Suite A
Minneapolis, MN 55419
800-216-0710
www.snowshoe.com

**Gil Gilpatrick (Outdoor books,
Master Maine Guide)**
P.O. Box 461
Skowhegan, ME 04976
207-453-6959
gil@gilgilpatrick.com
www.gilgilpatrick.com

INDEX

More Great Project Books from Fox Chapel Publishing

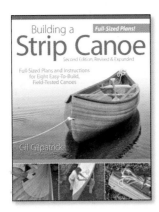

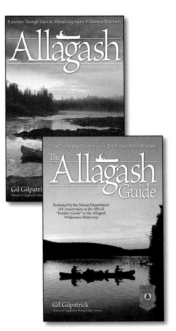

Building a Strip Canoe, 2nd Edition, Revised & Expanded
Full-Sized Plans and Instructions for Eight Easy-to-Build, Field-Tested Canoes
By Gil Gilpatrick

Paddle along with an expert outdoorsman and canoe builder as he shares his experience in guiding both novice and accomplished woodworkers in building a canoe with easy step-by-step instructions.

ISBN: 978-1-56523-483-3
$24.95 • 112 Pages

Building Wooden Snowshoes & Snowshoe Furniture
By Gil Gilpatrick

The art of making traditional wooden snowshoes and rustic snowshoe style furniture is given new life in this beautiful yet practical book by Gil Gilpatrick.

ISBN: 978-1-56523-485-7

$19.95 • 160 Pages

Allagash
A Journey Through Time on Maine's Legendary Wilderness Waterway
By Gil Gilpatrick

Expert Maine guide Gil Gilpatrick takes you on a journey down the awe inspiring Allagash River, skillfully weaving fact and fiction into fascinating stories about this legendary waterway.

ISBN: 978-1-56523-487-1
$19.95 • 232 Pages

The Allagash Guide
What You Need to Know to Canoe this Famous Maine Waterway
By Gil Gilpatrick

A book so extensively detailed about canoeing the Allagash River in Maine, by expert outdoorsman Gil Gilpatrick, it's like having him along for the trip.

ISBN: 978-1-56523-488-8
$11.95 • 104 Pages

Making Wooden Fishing Lures
Carving and Painting Techniques that Really Catch Fish
By Rich Rousseau

Whether it is the thrill of catching a fish with a handmade lure or finding a perfect lure to add to your collection, this book of 11 step-by-step projects with a collector's gallery will grab you hook, line, and sinker.

ISBN: 978-2-56523-446-8
$19.95 • 176 Pages

The Little Book of Whittling
Passing Time on the Trail, on the Porch, and Under the Stars
By Chris Lubkemann

Unwind while you learn to create useful and whimsical objects with nothing more than a pocket knife, a twig, and a few minutes of time.

ISBN: 978-1-56523-274-7
$12.95 • 104 Pages

WOODCARVING ILLUSTRATED

SCROLL SAW woodworking & CRAFTS

In addition to being a leading source of woodworking books and DVDs, Fox Chapel also publishes two premiere magazines. Released quarterly, each delivers premium projects, expert tips and techniques from today's finest woodworking artists, and in-depth information about the latest tools, equipment, and materials.

Subscribe Today!
Woodcarving Illustrated: **888-506-6630**
Scroll Saw Woodworking & Crafts: **888-840-8590**
www.FoxChapelPublishing.com

Visit CarvingPatterns.com for over 3,000 Original Patterns & Designs from Lora S. Irish.
Download patterns from the largest online library of original digital patterns and designs by artist L. S. Irish. Order, download, and be working on your next project all in the same day! If you are new to woodcarving, be sure to check out our FREE online tutorials and Beginner's Guide to Carving.